WHAT NEW CREATION?

WHAT NEW CREATION?

PAUL A. MICKEY & ROBERT L. WILSON

Abingdon

Nashville

WHAT NEW CREATION? THE AGONY OF CHURCH RESTRUCTURE
Copyright © 1977 by Abingdon

Library of Congress Cataloging in Publication Data

Mickey, Paul A 1937–
    What new creation?

    1. Church management. I. Wilson, Robert Leroy, 1925– joint
author. II. Title.
            BV652.M5   254   76-49559

                    ISBN 0-687-44850-6

Scripture quotations in the publication are from the Revised
Standard Version Common Bible, copyrighted © 1973.

The authors wish to express their appreciation to Editor James M.
Wall for permission to use quotations from *The Christian Century*.

MANUFACTURED BY THE PARTHENON PRESS AT
NASHVILLE, TENNESSEE, UNITED STATES OF AMERICA

Contents

PART II

The Religious Bureaucratic System

PART III

Changing the Bureaucracy

PART IV

Strategies for Managing the Bureaucracy

Preface

This is a book about the national Protestant bureaucracy, a subject on which almost every pastor and most lay people have strong and often negative opinions. Although the individual's knowledge of the denomination's national boards, agencies, instrumentalities, commissions, councils, or committees may be minimal, the feelings are clear and frequently expressed. What pastor has not complained about the volume of mail received from the national offices or the "handed-down" programs? What lay person has not questioned the cost of the denominational bureaucracy? How frequently has someone commented that agency staff members should "return to Christian work" by becoming pastors of congregations?

During the past decade the leaders of most Protestant denominations did more than talk about their national bureaucracy; they reorganized it. The term used to describe the process that began in the early 1960s and still continues a decade later is restructure. While hardly as exciting or newsworthy as clergy marching in civil rights or antiwar demonstrations, the reorganization of the denominational and ecumenical agencies is having a significant effect on the churches. Not only has the reorganization literally cost millions of dollars—money diverted from other causes—but it has resulted in major changes in the denominations.

The average person in the pew may hardly have been

aware that this reorganization was taking place. Those who knew probably did not care. Most lay members are usually content to trust the wisdom and judgment of the clergy and those lay persons who are delegates to the national church-governing bodies. The average pastor was aware that a reorganization was going on but tended to feel that the bureaucracy was getting a well-deserved shaking up.

Was the restructure of the national agencies important to the pastors and people in the local churches? The answer is an emphatic yes. The national church bureaucracy annually spends millions of dollars that have been put in the offering plates in churches across the nation. These organizations tend to determine the program emphases of the denomination. They produce the literature and the study books that influence the climate of opinion of the constituency. They determine which projects shall be recipients of mission funds. They control the means of communication and can decide which issues shall be brought to the attention of the constituency. They provide (or fail to provide) specialized services for the congregations such as leadership training, program planning, fund raising, counsel on erecting buildings, and so forth. The influence of the national agencies permeates church life.

The denominations need certain services that can best be provided by national agencies. These agencies are able to perform aspects of the church's witness and ministry that the local congregation cannot. Nevertheless, the potential and limitations of the national bureaucracy are not clearly understood by many persons associated with the agencies and by their constituencies. The bureaucrat is one of the most misunderstood church employees. A result of this lack of understanding is alienation, conflict, and a less effective witness and ministry. Both the bureaucrats and their constituents deserve better.

The major emphasis in this book will be on the restructure

of the national church agencies—why it occurred, how it was accomplished, what the immediate results have been, and what the implications are for the future. But while the focus is on the bureaucracy, the book is also about what is happening to the denominations which disassembled their national agencies and then put them back together in a different way. The picture is one of theological and institutional discontinuity.

The main focus of the study was on five major denominations: the American Baptist Churches, the Episcopal Church, the Presbyterian Church in the U. S., the United Presbyterian Church in the U. S. A., and The United Methodist Church. Limited information was gathered on other communions that had reorganized their bureaucracies.

The documents relating to reorganization were examined. The authors interviewed over 250 church leaders, both lay and clergy, who were involved in the process of restructure. Included were church executives, board members, and agency staff. Participants in the restructure process who favored and opposed the reorganization were interviewed.

The study was made possible by a research grant from the Reserve for Research, administered by the General Council on Ministries of The United Methodist Church.

This book has been made possible by the cooperation of many people. The authors are deeply endebted to the church leaders who make the records available and who generously gave their time to be interviewed. Especially valuable in arranging for interviewing was Warren Hartman and Doris Quinn of The United Methodist Church, Arthur Adams of the United Presbyterian Church U.S.A., James Andrews of the United Presbyterian Church in the U.S., and Harvey Everett of the American Baptist Churches. Appreciative gratitude is expressed for Divinity School staff assistance in the manuscript preparation, especially that of Jacquelyn P. Norris, and to Frances D. Parrish who typed the completed

11

manuscript with tender care. And finally the oft-unexpressed gratitude for family and student patience during the labors of love that came to be this book.

It is hoped that this book will contribute not only to more efficient denominational agencies but to a more effective ministry of the Christian Church.

PAUL A. MICKEY
ROBERT L. WILSON

PART I
The Predicament

Chapter 1
The Institutional Crisis

There was a time, not as long ago as it may now seem, when the world of the national Protestant bureaucracy seemed reasonably secure and even predictable. An invitation to join the staff of an agency was considered an honor. The work may have been demanding, but the staff members felt that they knew what was expected of them. The working relationships between the national agencies and their constituencies in the regional judicatories and local churches seemed clear. These conditions no longer exist. The national church agencies in the last decade have been through a period of drastic change during which most have been reorganized by their parent denominations (a process called restructure). Some agencies have been discontinued. Professional staff members, some with many years of service, have lost their positions or relocated into jobs not of their choosing.

Whether certain agencies or services should continue at all is the subject of continued debate. The claim is made by some that the old forms have been replaced with a new style of church bureaucracy to meet the needs of the present age. Other persons view the changes which have been and are occurring as essentially negative. They perceive less effective agencies engaging in activities inappropriate for the church. The result is an institutional crisis for the church

13

bureaucracy such as it has never before experienced in the United States.

This chapter will focus on the setting of the national church agencies, the rationale for their existence, and the symptoms of the current crisis.

The Setting of the Church Bureaucracy

Every denomination has several national agencies that are assigned tasks considered necessary or helpful to the local congregations or important for the fulfillment of the church's tasks. The organizations that have denomination-wide responsibility (in contrast to those limited to a regional judicatory such as a synod or an annual conference) constitute the national church bureaucracy.

The agencies are created by the governing body of the denomination, which determines their organizational structure, assigns tasks, and provides financial support. The denomination sets a procedure for the selection of a board of directors. A majority of members of the agency boards are elected by the regional judicatories according to a formula that insures the number is roughly proportional to the strength of the denomination in that area. In addition these directors may be authorized to select a specified number of persons "at large," which enables them to include members of minority groups and people with needed expertise. A requirement is some ratio of clergy and lay people and increasingly a definite proportion of women and members of minority groups. The board of directors is given the responsibility for overseeing the work of that agency. It is empowered to employ the staff who carry out the day-to-day work of the agency. The employees are directly responsible to the directors who in turn are responsible to the constituency of the denomination.

14

To be a member of a national board is generally considered an honor. Prominent clergy and lay persons have been elected most frequently to such offices. The position usually requires a considerable amount of time so that only persons who are able to give several weeks each year can adequately fill the major positions. Such service is voluntary (generally only the actual travel expenses to meetings are paid). The average employed person may not be able to serve because of the loss of income while away from the job.

The distinction between the board of directors and the staff is sometimes unclear. The board members are representatives of the denomination elected to direct the work of each agency. They employ the staff executives and set policies for the agencies. The board members usually vote on the employment of at least the top executives and often on the entire professional staff. The executives implement the policies and are authorized to employ additional persons such as lower-echelon professional staff, clerical workers, and others needed to carry out the work of the agency. The employed professional staff members are known as church bureaucrats.

The agencies that make up the national church bureaucracy may be multipurpose or single purpose. The multipurpose organizations, which constitute the majority, are those assigned a range of tasks. A social concerns agency, for example, may have responsibility for world peace, drug problems, labor relations, and population control. A home missions agency may be involved in maintaining schools for ethnic and language minorities, subsidizing pastors' salaries, and making loans to congregations for new buildings. Other agencies have only a single purpose such as providing for pensions for retired clergy or recruiting and certifying chaplains to serve in the armed forces.

Some parts of the church bureaucracy have been in existence for many years; others are of recent origin. The

15

number of employees will range from several hundred to only a few. The annual budgets will vary from a modest amount to millions of dollars.

The national church bureaucracy has fewer employees than is generally assumed (and the number has been decreasing). Considering the size of the membership of the denominations and the number of clergy and congregations in each, the total persons employed in the national agencies is not unusually large. The following statistics, which omit employees of the denominational publishing houses, illustrate the trend. The United Methodist Church with ten million members and twenty-five thousand clergy serving thirty-nine thousand congregations, has a national bureaucracy of about four hundred persons. The Episcopal Church with three million members, eleven thousand clergy, and seven thousand churches has had a decrease in the national staff from about one hundred forty in 1968 to less than forty in 1975. The Presbyterian Church in the U.S., a denomination with approximately a million members, four thousand congregations, and five thousand ordained clergy, has cut its agency staff during the past four years from about one hundred fifty to less than ninety.

Rationale for National Church Agencies

There are four reasons why Protestant denominations have national agencies. Virtually no one, either inside or outside of the church bureaucracy, objects to the validity of the first two. On the third there is not only a lack of consensus but sometimes violent disagreement. Many church people are not even aware of the fourth.

The first reason for the existence of national church agencies is to provide services necessary for the functioning of the local congregations and the welfare of the clergy. As

16

the denominations grew in size and as the expectations of the members rose, a range of resources were developed for use by people in the local churches. Foremost was printed material such as Bibles, tracts, books, Sunday school quarterlies, and subsequently records, cassette tapes, films, and filmstrips. The denominational publishing houses were organized to produce this literature for their constituency, a function they still perform. While there may from time to time be disagreement over the contents of the Sunday school literature, the validity or importance of the publishing enterprise is not questioned.

The number of services to local churches gradually increased. Agencies employ persons with expertise in a range of fields to assist congregations carry out their tasks. Fund raisers help churches conduct campaigns to solicit money. Counsel on building needs, architectural guidance, and loans to finance facilities are available. Research and planning services are provided. Resources and guidance assist congregations with their educational programs.

Services to clergy include the collection and investment of pension funds and the monthly payments to retired ministers, their widows, and any surviving dependent children. Some denominations provide placement services for clergy seeking a different parish. The tasks of recruiting and training new ministers and continuing education for pastors are promoted and supported by national church agencies.

A second reason for the existence of national agencies is to carry out a wide variety of ministries that are beyond the capabilities of the local congregation. Such ministries are considered a legitimate extension of the task of the local group and receive financial support from the constituency of the denomination.

The most obvious example has been the missionary enterprise. To take seriously the command to go into the world requires specialized organizations that can recruit and

17

train a force of missionaries and maintain them in the distant parts of the globe. Mission boards are among the oldest denominational agencies. As society increased in complexity, other specialized organizations were developed to carry out a variety of ministries. Foreign mission boards were followed by home mission agencies to minister to blacks, American Indians, and European and Oriental immigrants who were then settling in the large cities. Other activities with both an evangelistic and humanitarian motivation were established. These included homes for children, residences in large cities for single working women, settlement houses in urban slums, parochial schools for blacks in the Deep South and Spanish-speaking persons in the Southwest, and hospitals to serve underprivileged persons.

The financial support for these enterprises has come primarily from local congregations. Over the years some agencies have acquired endowments, often through bequests as interested individuals sought to perpetuate a particular work. There has been a constant attempt to make the individual church member feel a sense of identity with the agency's work. Probably the most effective means has been the missionary on furlough who travels from congregation to congregation explaining what he or she does and raising funds for its continuance.

Persons may disagree over what the mission of the church is, but virtually no one would limit the Christian witness only to the local congregation. No one would deny that a function of the denomination is to provide resources for the local congregation, although there may be some differences concerning which particular programs are most needed at a given time. Thus those agencies providing services to the congregation and clergy and those carrying on specialized ministries are acceptable to the constituency and receive continued support.

A third reason for the existence of the national agencies is to provide creative and trailblazing leadership that will move the denomination in directions that the constituency would not go if left alone. In the language of one period, the bureaucracy is to be the "cutting edge" of the denomination. The reasons for desiring change may be a new and different interpretation of the gospel or the mission of the church. It may be a current social problem to which some denominational leaders feel the church should respond. Nevertheless, lay persons and local pastors may be apathetic and unaware of the new understanding of the mission of the church. An issue that is considered a social problem or burning concern by the agency staff may not affect them directly. They may find the church as it now is quite adequate for their needs. Change, instead of being seen as desirable, may be viewed as a threat to the kind of church that has been meaningful to them.

Some national church agencies have been established to work for certain changes in the church and/or the larger society. This is usually due to the efforts of a strongly committed minority (although it may represent a majority of the denominational leaders). Such a new unit in the bureaucracy will have as one of its objectives educating or convincing the constituency to accept the newly defined goals.

A unit within the church bureaucracy established to lead the constituency in a direction they may not want to go will inevitably be involved in conflict. Such an organization, however, actually may tend to limit the level of conflict within the denomination. The social action agency thus provides an arena in which the issues can be clarified and differences resolved within the denominational family.

The individual expects that such an organization will work for social changes on which there will be disagreement. He can thus respond in a way that is appropriate for him.

19

Conflict may be prevented from becoming destructive by having an official forum for debate.

A fourth reason for having national church agencies is that they provide a political payoff for the clergy and lay person who faithfully serve the denomination in their home region. The person who has labored long, hard, and effectively in the vineyard known as the synod, association, presbytery, diocese, or annual conference may be appropriately rewarded with selection as director of a national agency. Such an individual becomes the spokesman for his region in the councils of the agency. At home he is recognized as a national leader in the far-off world of the national bureaucracy. One prominent layman who had served for many years as a director of his denomination's overseas mission board was known throughout his home judicatory as "Mr. Missions," a title he obviously relished.

The director of a national agency may be in a position to reward his or her friends with a staff position. While he may not in fact make the selection, he is in a position to know when vacancies will occur and to suggest and lobby for specific individuals. If the individual happens to be the chairman of the board or one of its major divisions or is a member of the executive committee, his power to dispense patronage is even greater. And the longer he serves as a director, the more he understands the working of the bureaucracy and how to manipulate it for his friends. Success in securing a staff position for a person from back home enhances the director's status in the eyes of his peers.

Every national church agency fulfills at least two of the four functions outlined above. Some agencies may perform all four. The same unit of the church bureaucracy may carry out ministries, provide some services for local congregations, and provide leadership which attempts to produce specific changes in both the church and society. At the same time it provides a method for rewarding the party faithful.

A home missions agency may provide direct services to congregations such as loans for church buildings, employ persons to be pastors in sparsely settled areas, and finance or employ community organizers in the black ghettoes. The result is a degree of conflict as segments of the constituency approve of some phases of the agency's work and disapprove of others. The level of conflict may escalate when an agency shifts its purpose from providing services to congregations to working for certain social changes. An example of this was the attempt by the United Methodist Board of Missions to use its endowment funds to dissuade a major bank from lending money to South Africa in protest of that nation's racial policy.

Symptoms of the Institutional Crisis

It is obvious that the national boards and agencies of the major Protestant denominations are in a state of crisis to anyone who will look carefully at these organizations. Some of the symptoms of the institutional crisis will be given here; others will be discussed in greater detail throughout the book.

1. *The Extent of Reorganizations:* In the 1960s and early 1970s virtually every denomination proceeded to dismantle its national bureaucracy and then reassemble it in a different manner. The rationale for this action varied; the results had striking similarities. One consequence has been a great deal of turmoil and lost motion as the time and effort of agency personnel have been expended on internal reorganization rather than on productive work.

A part of this process has been physical relocation of some units of the bureaucracy. Moving the offices seemed to symbolize that changes were in fact taking place. The Presbyterian Church in the U.S.A. relocated agencies from

21

Columbus, Ohio, and Philadelphia, Pennsylvania, to the Interchurch Center in New York City. The Presbyterian Church in the U.S. centralized its agencies in Atlanta, closing offices in Nashville, Tennessee, and Richmond, Virginia. The United Methodist Church engaged in a kind of bureaucratic musical chairs with the moving of a Philadelphia-based agency to New York in 1965–1967 and a series of changes in 1972 involving the relocation of some agencies from Chicago to New York and Nashville and the creation of a new unit located in the Chicago area. The overall effect was a greater concentration in New York and Nashville. Not included were relocations resulting from the merger of the Methodist and the Evangelical United Brethren denominations in 1968, which resulted in moves to and from Dayton, Ohio.

2. *Decrease of Financial Support:* The amount of money available to the national Protestant agencies has been declining. The pattern among the denominations has not been uniform; some have experienced a decrease in income while others have had some increase in support. The result has been a sharp cut in staff and program by certain organizations. Others have had periods of large operating deficits that have depleted reserves. The income of those agencies that have not had a decrease in the amount of dollars has not kept up with the rate of inflation.

The declining income has placed the church bureaucracy under considerable strain. Projects and institutions subsidized by the agencies have had their allocations cut. Staff has had to be reduced and life made more uncertain for those who remain. The result is increased anxiety among the employees and greater conflict over the diminishing financial resources. A subsequent chapter will be devoted to the financing of the church bureaucracy.

3. *Discontinuance of Well-Publicized Programs:* In the turbulent period of the 1960s some of the units within the

22

national church bureaucracy embarked on programs which were grandiose and costly. Some were launched with considerable publicity and heavy rhetoric. These were intended to have a significant effect on the larger society, generally with a goal of lessening the civil turmoil of that period.

While the motivation for such programs designed to promote social change may have been good, the wisdom and the effectiveness of such undertakings left much to be desired. Many of these enterprises were entered into in haste without careful consideration to their long-term effects on the institutions that sponsored them. While such programs were not designed to strengthen the churches, the extent to which they have weakened the agencies apparently was not anticipated. As a result, vast sums of money were expended with little or no evidence concerning what was in fact actually accomplished. Energies and resources were diverted from services and ministries to the traditional constituencies of the denominations. A decrease in the credibility of the church bureaucracies has had two results. The first has been a growing distrust in the national agencies by the constituents. The second has been an increasing degree of misgiving and sense of impotence by the bureaucrat as he sees his elaborate programs quietly fold.

4. *Limitations of Staff Tenure:* The lack of trust in the bureaucracy has come to focus on the professional staff. Some distrust of the bureaucrat by persons at the grass roots has always existed. The bureaucracy staff, however, has generally had the support of the denominational leaders both on the national level and in the regional judicatories. Even these persons are increasingly distrustful.

A limitation of tenure in staff jobs has been formally adapted by several denominations. The feeling seems to be that the staff executives simply cannot be trusted and therefore should only be hired for a limited period. One example is a denomination that permits staff to serve no more than three terms of three years each. At the end of nine years the person will have to leave, no matter how effective the individual's work has been. This is negatively affecting the morale of these persons held over from the old regimes and creating problems with the recruitment of new staff members. Individuals are reluctant to leave satisfying and significant positions for the increasingly uncertain and hostile world of the church agencies with a tenure policy that precludes the full maturing of a constructive new program under the person's care.

5. *Politization and Patronage:* The agencies are becoming the arena for open competition for patronage. The caucus groups within the denominations perceive staff positions in the national agencies as highly desirable, and great efforts are made to secure jobs for their members. This is most evident in the efforts of the caucuses to secure places on boards and staffs. When an opening occurs an attempt is made to see that it is filled by a black, Hispanic, Native American, Asian American, or a woman. Securing a position for a particular category of person becomes the end in itself. The process has resulted in an increasing degree of polarization and a de-emphasizing of the ministry or service that has been assumed to be the purpose of an assignment.

The level of conflict within the staffs has increased as groups struggle for patronage. The result has been a negative effect on both the achieving of the goals of the agency and on the morale of the persons involved.

6. *Confusion Over Purposes:* There is considerable confusion within some of the national Protestant agencies over their actual purpose. There is neither consensus among the staff, within the board of managers, nor throughout the general

24

constituency of the denomination concerning the purpose of a particular agency. While differences sometimes can be worked through to produce positive actions, there is evidence that the present situation may be producing bureaucratic immobility. Several agencies continue to reorganize in a kind of frantic search for some new form that will breathe purpose and meaning into their efforts.

The confusion over purpose is the most serious symptom of the current institutional crisis because it indicates lack of clarity about basic ideology. The functions of a church agency and the methods it employs are determined by its ideology, *i.e.*, its values and beliefs. Thus the form and function of an agency flow from its reason for being. How the funds are spent is directly related to the values it holds.

The ideology that has been foundational for the church bureaucracy has been shifting. Such changes are not always readily apparent to most faithful church people across the denominations, especially as they relate to bureaucratic operations and funding. Some bureaucrats themselves do not seem aware of the speed and nature of this change. No amount of attention to the structure itself or the rotation of staff members will automatically create a sense of purpose and clear goals.

The institutional crisis of the national Protestant bureaucracy is a symptom of a more serious difficulty. The basic problem is not one of organizational structure or management style, but of the values and ideology upon which the institution rests. The fundamental issue is theological. The next two chapters will examine the crises of belief and program.

Chapter 2

The Theological Crisis of Belief

National church agencies are a form of Christian ministry that help place the church in mission. Their mission and witness activities presuppose the prevailing theology of the church and the Daniel Boone phenomenon of leading the church into new territory. Hence the authority for any church activity is its theology. Granting this, what were the theological issues pertaining to reorganization? It is our contention that reorganization of the church agencies was a crisis of faith, not a crisis of organizational management and bureaucratic efficiency. This theological crisis was diffused and restated in secular, managerial, and organizational terms. Theological questions became organization and structure questions.

A subtle and profound shift occurred as lines of authority, responsibility, and accountability moved away from the witness of a denomination's doctrinal tradition. The contributions of scholars and theologians and the intuitive but often profound and stubbornly accurate theological expression of the laity shifted onto the shoulders of the bureaucracy. Staff believed that the church should make a relevant social witness, and the boards and agencies enjoyed considerable flexibility and financial independence in determining what courses they would follow. The energetic and creative

26

response to the cascading eruptions of urban, civil rights, peace, and hunger crises can only be applauded for its Christian intentionality. The crisis of faith was not precipitated by this kind of activity in itself. The real theological crisis was introduced by the intellectual and ideological sleight of hand which made virtue out of necessity. Gradually the denominations were guided by a novel ideology. This became a theology of *let the world set the agenda,* or let the world's ideology and politics become the church's theology.

One could imagine the dilemma as the relation of a steam engine to its train. The bureaucratic steam engine roared out of the station and into the world. Soon the church-in-general, the train, discovered it was *not* moving into the world. As this awareness dawned, the engine of bureaucracy was nearly out of sight. Clamor about the relationship arose and restructuring issued, but the precise theological issues remained obscured. In retrospect the real issue was not to devise a new technology to switch from steam to diesel power. Indeed, the issue was the way the engine was to be coupled to the train that carried the valuable cargo of the historic tradition, educated and dedicated ministers, resident theologians, doctrinal standards, and grass-roots, local congregations. What connects the bureaucratic engine to the church-in-general is not program but theology. Bona-fide programs are in actuality the progress of the entire train or church. Theology is what keeps it together and apart.

The crisis of faith cannot be displaced and relocated into organizational structures. Churches need to examine theological assumptions as well as the bureaucratic programs if the national churches of the 1970s and 1980s are not to find themselves repeating the theological weather-vaning of the 1960s. Fresh winds of the city and "fresh winds of the Spirit" both require thoughtful theological evaluation. In an effort to illustrate this theological crisis of faith we surveyed *The Christian Century* from January, 1960, through December,

27

1973. This periodical has been considered a truly ecumenical religious journal in the United States and therefore is a general theological barometer for that period. Our rationale for this procedure was corroborated by *The Christian Science Monitor*.[1]

The *Monitor* survey was focused on seminarians, and while this does not prove a bureaucratic readership, it suggests that the early established reading habits persist. As a barometer, *The Christian Century* reflected and reinforced the interests, moods, and perspectives of the national agency staff whether or not specific staff were subscribers. Further, those of the various national agencies who related to the church-related press would generally be comfortable with *The Christian Century* as a general ecumenically oriented periodical. Our hypothesis does not rest upon a subscriber list but upon a relative professional homogenity of staff perspective and *The Christian Century* ideological and marketing focus.

Ecumenics and Missions: The True Church Visible or Invisible

The debate over the true nature and the function of the church became sharply divided during the period 1960–1973. Is the church to direct its life toward increasing its power and visibility as an institution, or is the church to submerge like

---

[1] *The Christian Century* (January 14, 1970), p. 37. "It is therefore a matter of some satisfaction to note the recent survey of the views and reading habits of today's seminary students reported in *The Christian Science Monitor* by that paper's religious affairs editor, Louis Garinger. The survey found that the *Century* is 'the most widely read religious publication' among the seminarians and is third among all publications read by them, following *Time* and *Newsweek*. After the *Century* came the *New York Times*, *Life*, the *New Republic*, the *National Catholic Reporter*, *Christianity Today*, *Christianity and Crisis*, and *Theology Today*."

yeast in the bread of other sociological agencies? If the latter, which from among a limitless number of possible mixes should be selected? By December, 1973, a definitive decision was not available. But the battle between high and low visibility, small and large power groupings, had raged and with some significant consequences.

Initially a call to move from nationalism to theism was proclaimed. *The Christian Century* urged its readers to set aside the notion "that the chosen people will be Americans or at least Christian Americans," and urged them to overcome "our various Protestant denominations."[2] Charles C. Morrison echoed this concern: "Our churches consist in our imposing, alien, man-made sectarian ecclesiastical structures upon these parish churches as well as between them and the one true church of Christ." He observed that the Protestant bureaucracy *stands between* the local church and the true church, blocking communication and the truth. ("These activistic, business-like 'jobs' are filled mainly by former parish ministers who are too easily tempted by the quasi-secular character of such jobs.") Thus, "the denomination as church is such an illegitimate intermediate," its visibility obstructs the true (ecumenical) church.[3] Opening further the thrust of this argument in a brief review of Philippe Maury's book *Politics and Evangelism*, William Danker questioned the value "of employing salaried clergy," arguing from sociologist Max Weber that "the bureaucratic element has crowded out the charismatic."[4] Theologically, his concern was to affirm the work of the Holy Spirit outside the institutional structures and to challenge the church on its false visibility and stifling spirituality.

[2] "National Purpose and Christian Mission," editorial, *Christian Century* (January 6, 1960), p. 3.

[3] "The Nature of Protestant Disunity," *Christian Century* (March 9, 1960), p. 283.

[4] "Mission and the Holy Spirit," review of *Politics and Evangelism* by Phillipe Maury, *Christian Century* (February 15, 1961), p. 209.

Unity Vs. Diversity. By contrast, J. V. Casserley argued for a visible continuity of apostolic ministry.[5] Methodist bishop Gerald Kennedy worried about organic unity, stating that we can have unity in the best sense without an organic unity of the Protestant churches. Episcopal layman William Stringfellow warned against compulsive organizing: "The secret of Christian unity which is revealed in the case of the Christian for the world, is the presence of the Word of God already in the common life of the world . . . there is the radical and integral relationship of all men and all things."[6] Here the debate is about organizational (*i.e.,* church-type and sect-type) unity and theological diversity within Christendom. These leaders would contend that there can be no unity without diversity. God in his grace is present equally in diversity and not necessarily more so in organizational unity. So ecumenical structures were not a required answer.

A New Worldliness. William Danker observed among Asian Christians that the contemplative spiritualism of Hinduism and Buddhism has influenced western theology: "the holier a Christian becomes, the less he should be concerned for a secular society."[7] Thus, the Christian needs to "erase the artificial distinction between the sacred and the secular and recognize that all of life is holy and belongs to the Lord." The thrust is that the church must recognize the actuality of the sacred and secular as equal in God's providence and correct its theology to reflect this. Correspondingly, later articles stressed the "servanthood of the

---

[5] "The Apostolic Ministry," *Christian Century* (April 5, 1961), p. 420.

[6] "The Secret of Christian Unity," *Christian Century* (September 13, 1961), pp. 1073-76.

[7] "Two Worlds or None," *Christian Century* (June 5, 1963), p. 737.

laity" and the imperative of urban "laos parishes."[8] The "new missionary" utilized a Peace Corps model being "liberal, practical, secular."[9] Many were eager to move away from traditional, institutional, religious, spiritual modes of church mission. Stephen Rose argued openly for this style: "At the outset, I believe, we must also accept the fact that beyond the local church level, the fundamental organization is bureaucratic."[10] He called for a new highly visible ecumenical structure that would have real power. Rose noted that "talent moves toward the greatest possibility for the exercise of creative power." He concluded: "The central point is that authority and ecumenicity must converge. There can be no effective ecumenicity without effective power."[11] Thus, he wanted a centralization of function through organic unity to acquire secular power. Aware that tradition, institutions, and bureaucracy are necessary for power and that power is necessary to function, Rose drew back from advocating a nonworldly ecumenicity. He was reluctant to abandon the church as a viable, visible institution.

One more perspective on worldliness in missions and ecumenics was well expressed by Per Lønning:

> Certainly "church and society" problems can hardly be solved by simply saying that the church, without claiming anything for itself, exists to serve the secular society. The idea underlying this statement—that Christ is the servant and incognito—lacks meaning unless it is combined with a proclamation of Christ as the Risen Lord. If Christ came only to serve in humility and anonymity, his logical goal could only have been oblivion. And if his main activity today is to set man free through the processes of "desacralization" and secularization, and if he refuses to claim

---

[8]John Fry, "United Presbyterians: Prophecy vs. Tradition," *Christian Century* (October 9, 1963), pp. 1235-37.

[9]"Methodist Missions Retooled," special report, *Christian Century* (October 14, 1964), p. 1273.

[10]"Proposals for Uppsala," *Christian Century* (September 6, 1967), pp. 1123-26.

[11]*Ibid.*, p. 1125.

authority over the thoughts of men, the most efficient contribution that the church could make to his mission would be to stop talking about him.[12]

Stephen Rose wanted to apply his concern for "real power" in the World Council of Churches (WCC) and the Consultation on Church Union (COCU). A worldly power in visible form was central. At root was the dilemma that the church needs power to be a servant, yet it distrusts that power for theological reasons. The bureaucratic tendency is to fight to claim the power; the theological assessment is to distrust or scrutinize that visible power. As Rose suggested, to be a powerful bureaucracy is an alluring goal—especially when theological correctives are brought into play.[13]

A New Inwardness. Alarm over several of the recently formed conservative movements in U.S. Protestantism was expressed by Aubrey Haines. These groups appeared as divisive and polarizing to him. He contrasted their "faith theology" against "works theology." The conservatives would call for a visible faith, whereas Haines saw the mainline position supporting a faith visibly at work, but the "works" were not a substitute for faith.[14] Such artificial polarizations, warned Haines, would be destructive for all.

Expressing further this concern about polarization, United Methodist pastor Harold Bosley said:

The churches' concern for social issues is alienating many of the older generation of churchmen without winning the support of an appreciable number of those—younger and older alike—who,

[12]"The Theological Basis for the Geneva Conference," *Christian Century* (March 1, 1967), p. 271.

[13]"Process and Power—The Lineaments of Valid Ecumenical Unification," *Christian Century* (February 25, 1970), p. 233.

[14]"Polarization Within the Churches," *Christian Century* (September 2, 1970), pp. 1039-41.

while deeply concerned about social issues, refuse to get involved in the churches.[15]

Frustration deepened as the current theology of ecumenics and missions struggled to relate secular and sacred, local and world. Church bureaucracies claim servanthood and selfless service, but they tend to practice Stephen Rose's dictum that visible power is the proper administrative style. This shift found support in "revolutionary" theology that would call for massive engagement and confrontation with secular structures. Once committed to power confrontation theology, the bureaucracy turned inward from selfless witness to arm for battle with secular structures. Confrontation theology cannot embrace both secular and sacred; again, the world sets the agenda. Each battle a new agenda: which massive political or economical windmill will the church bureaucracy attack next? As Don Quixote, the bureaucracy rides off to battle secular windmills; the poor ass upon which the institutional warrior is riding—the local church—is threatening to balk.

This problem is not simply that of localism. The local church is being spurred to death while the quixotic bureaucracy compulsively fights each passing windmill, seeing it as a prophetic vision or encounter. Dean Kelley called this orientation "The Un-Service Station," arguing that the bureaucracy is not supplying the churches the product or services their members need.[16] Based on Kelley's assessment it is little wonder that congregations and denominational bureaucracies are frustrated by each other. Timothy Miller has inadvertently laid bare the problem:

> In recent years there has been talk among Christians of "abandonment" and "the church losing itself." . . . True abandonment is still far away—because it really means giving up the

---

[15] "The Quiet Storm in the Churches," *Christian Century* (December 2, 1970), p. 1449.

[16] "The Un-Service Station," *Christian Century*, (June 30, 1971), p. 799.

deep-seated biases that prohibit truly disinterested service to other persons. It means foregoing the self-righteous label of "Christian" when we serve in the world.[17]

If one cannot be a Christian in order to be of service, then as Per Lønning argued, we might as well stop talking about Christian service. Selfless service, yes; but a disinterested service with no allegiance beyond service for service's sake could hardly be called Christian or church service. No service is void of motivation. If service occurs, some motivation is at the root of the act. An appeal to disinterested service to supplant selfless Christian service cuts loose the church's activities from its tradition, doctrine, people, and vocation—all being necessary theological moorings. In a critique of COCU Dennis Campbell expressed the dilemma: "The *real* issue facing Protestantism is not organizational ecumenism but faithfulness to the gospel."[18] Christian service witness and faithfulness to the gospel call one to selfless service but *not* "disinterested" service. The two tend to be mutually exclusive! The bureaucracy, by and large, looked for disinterested service, the parish congregation for faithfulness embodied in service.

The Pendulum of Radical Doubt and Faith

The period 1955–1975 was a time of unprecedented swings in theological mood and orientation, with 1960–1970 a time of great instability. These faith tremors were released by the recognition (1) that the church was not infallible as an institution, (2) that leaders required scrutiny, and (3) that many persons yearned for a stable personal religion. In this

---

[17]"Cosmological Christology and the Missionary Impulse," Readers' Response, a regular column in *Christian Century* (January 12, 1972), p. 43.

[18]"COCU and the Future: Is the Consultation Doomed?" *Christian Century* (August 16, 1972), p. 821.

period a concurrent convulsive experience of the degradation of institutions and personal faith occurred. There was no sustaining object of worship.

The Demise of Christendom. In a review article, "Recessional for Christendom," and in a subsequent article Martin Marty proclaimed the demise of the church as an institution.[19] "I like to invert John R. Mott's phrase about 'Evangelizing the world in our generation' and speak of 'Enworlding the evangel in our generation.'" From Bonhoeffer he secured the counterpoint, a "world come of age." The secular was to enworld the evangel. It was time for seminarians to stop hiding behind institutional Christendom and enworld themselves. This keynote spawned a generation of anti-institutional seminarians and bureaucrats.

Culbert Rutenber grasped the import of this theme, warning that the theologians were "so busy transferring God from the church to the world" that they saw "the hand of God too quickly in the things we would like to believe are God's acts, thus cutting off further analysis and inhibiting further understanding."[20] This blocked a needed critique of the church and produced an impulsive desire to reform the church. Bishop John A. T. Robinson stated this critique in profoundly insightful and disturbing terms in *Honest to God.* Far from claiming a simple atheism that would declare that the world is the object of faith, Robinson wanted a "worldly holiness" whose center of faith was, of course, Jesus Christ. Some were critical of the lack of a well-developed Christology to support the bishop's "religionless society," noting that the

---

[19]"Recessional for Christendom," *Christian Century* (January 6, 1960), pp. 13-15; "Bonhoeffer—Seminarians' Theologian," *Christian Century* (April 20, 1960), pp. 467-69.

[20]"No Access to God's Diaries," *Christian Century* (December 22, 1965), pp. 1570.

study should have been entitled "Honest to the Church." [21] A misreading of Robinson at this point provided further fuel for an antichurch and antitranscendence reaction which advocated the collapse of church establishment more than faithful service in the name of Jesus Christ.

Jacques Ellul observed this theological double bind: If overthrowing church structures is a goal, an "overthrow of the basic, actual structures of the modern world" becomes impossible. The church is caught between chaos and paralysis. Breaking the double bind is most difficult: It "cannot be accomplished save by starting with the individual's discovery by himself." [22]

A church that is secularized, subdued, and anti-Christendom cannot be the church. Lutheran pastor Richard Neuhaus observed of the destructive mood of the period: "So too, only those who care about the worshiping community have the right to speak out in the *name of the church* on behalf of the oppressed." [23] Many, like Neuhaus, who remained active in local parishes could fault themselves, their church, and their activities in the sixties, but in honoring the worshiping community they would go on. A similar commentary was offered by Baptist pastor Robert Seymour who criticized the leadership of the Ecumenical Institute of Chicago as rigid, antiquated, vestigial fundamentalism. These pastors suggested that genuine church reform does not come by destructive demise of the objects of faith. By the early 1970s pastors and laity alike were rediscovering the centrality of "objects of faith" for church life. But funding priorities of the national Protestant boards and agencies gave

---

[21] "Honest to the Church," editorial, *Christian Century* (May 8, 1963), pp. 603-4.

[22] "Between Chaos and Paralysis," *Christian Century* (June 5, 1968), p. 749.

[23] "The Loneliness of the Long-Distance Radical," *Christian Century* (April 26, 1972), p. 481.

little indication of a similar discovery of and care about the church as a worshiping community.[24]

The tensions of the 1960s pushed the poles of faith and doubt farther apart, creating ever-increasing tension in the churches' claim for unity and wholeness in Christian life and responsibility. Efforts to claim a middle ground, wholeness, unity, integration, peace, growth, and goodwill fell on difficult times. Eventually wholeness and unity toward community turned inward to a protection of self interests. A further development of this collapse of wholeness was to project one's felt inferiority onto other persons and groups. Thus, wholeness became inwardness.

The review of Martin Heidegger's *Being and Time* by William Hordern indicates this cleavage and collapse:

> But there seems to be no reason why man cannot achieve Heidegger's authentic life by himself. In fact, Heidegger's view of authentic life sounds much like what the Reformation called the sin of man's being curved in on himself . . . Heidegger's authentic man bathes perpetually in the joy of being guilty . . . In fact, nothingness is virtually worshiped as a saving god.[25]

Hordern detected a profound alienation in Heidegger's work and influence. Where are the positive, supportive, nurturing corporate relationships in the authentic life? The sociality and corporateness of Christian life, the body of Christ appears diminished. Hence, we find radical faith in the doubt that mankind can achieve wholeness. For Heidegger this would have been active sinning. His language supports a passivity that turns in upon itself.

Claude Welch endeavored to counteract retreat into inwardness. He claimed that theological presuppositions must undergird the action of faith.

---

[24]"Prepackaged Religion," *Christian Century*, (September 20, 1972), pp. 922-23.

[25]"Heidegger: King Without Clothes," *Christian Century*, (December 5, 1962), p. 1482.

Yet it is precisely this situation that raises the question of possibility and significance of any Christian faith at all; faith's most fundamental affirmations concerning the reality of its object have to be critically explicated. And that means a theological turn (or return) from anthropological preoccupations to the doctrine of God.[26]

The center of inwardness is mankind; the center of faith is God. Accompanying this radical faith in man was a radical doubt in God. Thomas A. J. Altizer wrote: "A theology which continues to proclaim the reality of God is closed to the contemporary reality of the incarnation."[27] Could one have theology both ways: radical faith in man, radical doubt in God?

Leory Howe said it straightaway:

What should be alarming about the death of God movement is not its gospel, which is hardly news anymore, but rather its stark illustration of the deficiency within Protestantism that is seldom honestly faced: the absence of external criteria for judgments about the inner, spiritual life. This issue is my concern here. My thesis is: radical theology brings to completion a Protestantism, bereft of a logic of faith, and it can be overcome only by transcending every appeal to inwardness as the ultimate criterion for determining what is the Christian message.[28]

The bureaucracy seemed to advocate this upside-down cake theology: faith in humanity and doubt in God. In theological circles, however, some of the slippage into inwardness was changing by the end of this era. In 1969 Charles West saw radical politics potentially moving beyond the new inwardness:

[26]"Theology as Risk," *Christian Century* (June 2, 1965), p. 708.
[27]"Creative Negation in Theology," *Christian Century* (July 7, 1965), p. 864.
[28]"Radical Theology and the Death of Discourse," *Christian Century* (May 3, 1967), p. 583.

As every radical community soon discovers, the problem of human community is not solved by liberating human beings from their inhibitions for the sake of self-discovery. History remains an intractable problem as long as human power exists.[29]

Put bluntly, radical politics had to risk history. It was not a license to fondle the "self-discovery." Royal Shepard named four tendencies in the contemporary milieu which had facilitated the slippage from wholeness to inwardness to fanaticism:

1) *negativity*—the tendency to live by what one rejects, not what one affirms,

2) *vagueness*—a reluctance to be definite in matters of doctrine,

3) *indecisiveness*—the Hamlet-like quality of rhetorical overkill, and

4) *relativism*—or "to-a-certain-extentism"—the feeling that nothing should be too strongly believed.[30] Of such ideological bulwarks would the kingdom of the bureaucracy be built in the early sixties. The rains of radical doubt and faith fell upon that house melting it into the soft sands of a radical inwardness, sometimes called faith.

Against the inwardness moved that venerable workhorse of social witness and responsibility, Reinhold Niebuhr. He acknowledged the age of secularism by declaring that "we are dealing with a system of meaning for which no irrefutable rational proof can be given but to which we must bear witness by the quality of our lives." And that is accomplished he argued,

In our congregations, whose integral community is one of the real achievements of the American sectarian and immigrant church,

---

[29] "Returning to Nature," review of *A Theology for Radical Politics* by Michael Novak, *Christian Century* (July 30, 1969), p. 1021.

[30] "Faith, Freedom and Fanaticism," *Christian Century* (November 14, 1973), pp. 1123-25.

authentic witness can only mean that we are to save them from triviality, religiosity and uncreative "chumminess" by transmuting them into real communities of grace where the individual is "completely known and all forgiven," and where his individual work in its dignity and weakness is guarded against the perils of dehumanization inherent in the technical impersonality of an industrial civilization.[31]

Fully aware of the danger of a vacuous piety and the dehumanizing technology, Niebuhr urged the church to reaffirm its task to participate actively in bringing about real communities of grace. This could only be accomplished in a communal setting. Niebuhr's concern for the social dimensions of humanity was often misinterpreted by a mind-set that stressed the "species goodness" of mankind thereby affirming personal license but not God's grace. This orientation was "an exaggerated confidence in the goodness of men and in the redemptive nature of history," declared W. Kenneth Cauthen. He spoke in support of Niebuhr's "realism":

The heart of the matter is that the liberal notion of an immanent Spirit at work gradually imparting order to nature and by an evolutionary process bringing man to moral and spiritual perfection within history is too simple a version of the relationship between man, the world, and God.[32]

The Niebuhr–Cauthen challenge to active involvement in the system of justice in social and corporate arenas was turned aside for idealism and a naïve optimism. The harsh realism of civil rights violence, national political convention fights, and the peace movement caught the soft underbelly of anthropological and sociological idealism by surprise. Quick retreat became the order of the day.

The dynamics of the retreat to inwardness can be

[31] "The Quality of Our Lives," *Christian Century* (May 11, 1960), p. 572.
[32] "Religious Liberalism Evaluated," *Christian Century* (August 8, 1962), p. 957.

symbolized by Philip Rieff's *Triumph of the Therapeutic*.[33] The therapeutic person, or "psychological man," is one released from communal tyranny. ("The new psychological man," Rieff contended, "will be relatively detached from communal purpose.") Detachment, noninvolvement, playing it cool, and hanging loose were the characteristics of this new creation. This movement from release to detachment was a profound shift in self-understanding. Location of one's identity shifted from social and communal to internal and intrapsychic moorings. Horace Greeley's adage "Go West, young man" underwent a rapid reversal. A new, Rieffian adage might be "Go East, young man." Eastward toward meditation, dropping out, transcendentalism the "psychological man" went, especially the youth. But one does not remain unattached for long. There must be an object of regard and esteem even if it is the universe in general or emptiness in general, or Nirvana. Concentration on "emptiness" was more affirming ultimately than detachment from everything.

Among the church bureaucracy the movement probably was more inward than eastward, but the withdrawal dynamics from social expansion was common in church and culture. The bureaucrat is bound intrinsically to social, corporate, and communal structures and styles of power and life. One cannot simply drop out. But turning in was a real mood and move. Suddenly the likes of National Training Labs, sensitivity training, conflict management, group process, and long periods of group and staff process were the bureaucratic symbolization of turning from the field to the retreat centers and staff preoccupation with, if not meditation upon, itself and its detachment from communal purpose.

The detachment and distance from emotionality, psychological, and theological spontaneity in the bureaucracy

---

[33] Don Browning, "Restrained Release," review of *The Triumph of the Therapeutic* by Philip Rieff, *Christian Century* (April 13, 1966), p. 465.

prevented the bureaucrats from delving into mysticism, the charismatic movement (especially healing and tongues-speaking services), and, in general, those activities that involved a deep personal releasing. This was too close to home and too hot to handle. The entire Jesus movement and the charismatic scene were "off limits." Many bureaucrats came from backgrounds that could not accommodate such activities. The residual conflict and, therefore, anger toward the old pietism was too near the surface to permit contemporary acceptance. The bureaucrat was more identified with rationality and comptrollers. This threat was deep indeed. Many other groups and movements had been acknowledged and affirmed by the national church bureaucracies. But, by 1975 no one had been hired on a national bureaucracy because he or she was a mystic, tongues-speaker, or faith healer.

The bureaucracy, however, did not miss a good market opportunity. Representatives of these groups were granted some visibility and bureaucratic sanction. They participated on a very selective basis in agency-sponsored programs. This was more or less like the returning military veteran participating in the War Department's effort to sell war bonds; it appeared glorious on the surface, but there was little personal value for the veteran raising funds and prestige for someone else. The principal dynamic was the bureaucracy's withdrawal from aggressive involvement in the field. A total inwardness was not a live option for the bureaucrat. A compromise ensued. The bureaucracy's anthropology bobbed around in the "therapeutic man" life raft in midstream, living in its own little world and certain not to arrive at either social or inward ports of entry.

During the period theological discussion remained in vogue but shifted in value. It was not seen as the basis for church programming rationale because it assumed a more diminutive and compartmentalized function. The specific if not peculiar theological distinctives of the various special interest or pressure groups were recognized and honored at least as being worthy of debate, argument, and funding. But theology in general—that is, systematic theology—was not vigorously and decisively joined. Eventually it was courted in its "comeback" in the early 1970s but more as a parlor room conversation piece—a polite, diminutive dialogue. Theology simply was not the "name of the game" for the bureaucracy.

Chapter 3
The Theological Crisis of Program

Having explored the theological crisis of beliefs, we now turn to program activities. The concern is not to examine particular activities for explicit theological content, but to consider two general areas of theological discourse that undergird program philosophy and emphasis: theological mood and the slippery consensus over missional relevancy.

In the first instance, traditional American optimism has suffered painful alterations. Optimism is a theological theme from which the church draws energy and ideas for programming priorities.

Secondly, the desperate cry to the church to engage in struggles for human equality and justice awakened a sleeping giant. Once awakened, the church had to ask about the principle of limitation for involvement.

Optimism and Pessimism in Theology

The general theological background for American optimism regarding self-sufficiency was the Puritan doctrine of the sovereign efficacy of Divine Providence: "God hath the absolute infallible termination of the success and benefits" of all human activities because man, being "absolutely depen-

44

dent" upon God for his being, could not know directly God's will. The declared dependency became the subtle philosophical rootage of pragmatism and provisionalism of a Puritan-derived theology. To believe in the doctrine of Providence was to be a pragmatist. God's will would be expressed, not in particular revelations to individuals but in the total picture, the general pattern, the "success" of history, and among the chosen who were destined to participate in this success.[1]

The "Readers' Response" for March 28, 1962, argued for theological pluralism from the "dark face of God" vantage. Benjamin Miller said, "The supernaturalistic claim to be a religion of revelation is exclusive and divisive." He further stated, "The core of the historic Christian community essentially has been moral and liturgical rather than theological." Gradually what became normative was not the faith *received* and *discovered*, "but the practice and the celebration of the way of love toward the mutual self-fulfillment of persons as persons."[2] Personal fulfillment replaced God's providence. Human potential and power were becoming the theological focal points. The difficulty arose following the relocating of theological optimism from God's providence to human potential when the authority and power of the church was, likewise, seriously challenged.

For example, when the "oughtness" of religious institutions was under attack, Roger Hazelton observed: "Some form of social structure with its attendant perils, some way of effecting and transmitting our 'life together' in Christ, is not only right but absolutely indispensable to Christian mission and witness in the world. ... Certainly long-overdue changes in the patterns of Christian believing and behaving will result from this stirring of new life, but such changes will

---

[1] William Smith, "The Dark Face of God," *Christian Century* (May 18, 1960), p. 600-602.

[2] Benjamin Miller, Readers' Response, *Christian Century* (March 28, 1962), p. 400-402.

not be its cause."[3] The church as an institution is necessary; but optimism about institutions, for the tradition of the faith received and discovered, was subjected to intense pressure.

In 1972 two articles pressed the optimism issue. Niebuhr suggested "The Not-So-Moral Man in His Less Moral Communities" as a "revised" title for his classic work *Moral Man and Immoral Society.* The conflicts produced by one's own reference or power-base group located in society, will persist.[4] More power begets potentially more evil. Church bureaucracy, as a society, is potentially more sinful than the sins it seeks to overcome. It is both less and more than its theological vision.

An optimistic view toward God's providence, located in social and institutional programs, became secularized and withdrawn.

The erosion of an optimism toward the object of faith, God, and the ensuing negativity distressed sociologist Peter Berger with regard to the active interpretation of civil religion in the civil rights and Vietnam peace movements. These movements had become so critical and radical that he registered his own protest: "The task of the churches today may not be just one of 'radical' criticism, and certainly not one of legitimating revolution. No, the task of the churches today is to call back our society to what is best (I would even say to what is God-given) in its values, including its political ideals."[5]

Some Secondary Themes: Saul Alinsky, the Evangelicals, and the Parish. The community organizer Saul Alinsky, an

---

[3]"The Holy Spirit and Religion," *Christian Century* (January 20, 1965), pp. 73-74.

[4]Tracy Early, "Reinhold Niebuhr for the '70s," *Christian Century* (June 14, 1972), pp. 688-90.

[5]"Between Tyranny and Chaos," *Christian Century* (October 30, 1968), p. 1365.

aggressive social activist, was never an editorial favorite of *The Christian Century*, which expressed its editorial concern that the real leaders whom Alinsky *et al.* had in mind (lower-class Negroes) "reject politics as Americans understand it; they reject relief, recreation and social agencies, and probably the churches, as dispensers of barbiturates."[6] While Alinsky could not be seen as a church leader or theologian, response to his effective, pragmatic approach to social and community action was an indication of some church leaders' actual willingness to be socially involved. Alinsky, through the Industrial Areas Foundation (IAF), argued that the democratic system either had never been introduced or had broken down. Hence, conflict had to be introduced to create a new order. *Christian Century* recoiled, "This running of a society and a state, we are told, is more important than electing good men to office and throwing out the rascals."[7] Fearful of Alinsky's capacity to trigger undemocratic procedures through self-initiated conflict for specific, pragmatic goals, *Christian Century* remained suspicious and hostile. Subsequently this view represented a common reaction to Alinsky's advocacy of public conflict.[8] It was difficult to sacrifice universal application to achieve immediate, contextual goals; Alinsky's realism was too pragmatic. A true optimistic secularist, Alinsky could get things done. Church secularists generally spoke secular ideology but not secular action, secular rhetoric but not simple realism. Finally in 1971 Stephen Rose interviewed Alinsky for *The Christian Century* and penned a eulogy, "Taps for a Radical." He wrote: "Alinsky helped me to see

---

[6] "Revolution—What Kind?" editorial, *Christian Century* (July 18, 1962), p. 880.

[7] *Ibid.*, p. 880.

[8] "Thank You, No; Mr. Alinsky," editorial, *Christian Century* (June 2, 1965), p. 701; "The Greatest Good for All," editorial (June 30, 1965), pp. 827-28; "With Such Friends," editorial (September 1, 1965), pp. 1052-53.

(though I did not always take it to heart) that personal conviction no matter how righteous, is no substitue for an honest assessment of what one really wants to achieve and what one is willing to sacrifice to achieve it." [9] *The Christian Century's* perception of and relation to Saul Alinsky was a sensitive indicator of the church's confusion over the difference between idealistic secular rhetoric and realistic secular action.

Relations between *The Christian Century* and the evangelicals continued to deteriorate and become abrasive during this period. In January, 1961, there was evidence of an appreciative relationship between the two groups. In commenting on the death of Donald Grey Barnhouse and the integrity of his ministry and editorship of *Eternity* magazine, *The Christian Century* said: "But in Dr. Barnhouse we saw the newer evangelicalism at its finest." [10] The differences in theological approach were illustrated by John Lawson's review of Kenneth Cauthen's *Impact of American Religious Liberalism.* The evangelical, in Lawson's words, would appeal to "the objective atonement" as theological truth whereas the liberal would appeal to "the natural world and human life in it as a continuous process. . . . that God is immanent in the process" as theological truth. Thus, there was a major theological difference between the evangelical sentiment, "Let the water and the blood,/From thine riven side which flowed," and an appeal to let the world set the agenda. The latter expressed a "theology without Grace." [11]

The lack of charity continued during the period and could be illustrated by a brief exerpt from a column entitled

---

[9] "Discerning Power Realities," *Christian Century* (May 19, 1971), pp. 622-26; "Taps for a Radical" (July 5, 1972), p. 736.

[10] "Neo-Evangelical Politics," editorial, *Christian Century* (January 4, 1961), pp. 4-5.

[11] "Theologies Without Grace," *Christian Century* (January 2, 1963), p. 15.

"Evangelical Calendar": "July 20 is the 'first man on the moon' day, which every latter-day fundamentalist knows honors the greatest week since creation."[12] This note symbolized mutual distance—and distrust—within mainline denominations.

Finally, we noted the ambivalence about parish ministry. A quick glance at the booksellers' ads in *The Christian Century* showed that preaching and counseling were very popular early in the sixties. By May, 1966, a lead editorial sentence announced: "The suburban ministry has lost its attractiveness for many theological students." There followed a military-type recruiting poster statement appealing to volunteers for a dangerous mission in the suburban parish. The secular city was luring persons from suburbia and the parish church. This concern was explored by Browne Barr who argued that the role of the minister in revolutionary times is essentially the same as it is in other times. Barr was not concerned about the geographical location or sociological profile of the parish but rather its character, which he argued "is determined by its gospel. So preach the gospel, administrate the sacraments, and bear rule in the church . . . What is called for is not right doctrine but right faith."[13] For Barr ideology and rhetoric were less important than to be a faithful witness in preaching, sacraments, and discipline. What had captivated the bureaucracy was revolution, not faithfulness. In a period of incredible confusion, revolution was more appealing than tradition.

Changing Consensus About Relevancy

American Protestantism approached the end of the fifties noticing the hairline cracks in the veneer of the universality

---

[12]"Pen-Ultimate," *Christian Century* (February 10, 1971), p. 207.

[13]"Bury the Parish?" *Christian Century* (February 15, 1967), p. 199.

of the affluent middle class that soon would erupt into open conflict. The early sixties brought a new and painful awareness of the frightfully oppressed in both urban and rural settings.[14] Pricked by its complacency of the fifties, the church bureaucracy responded but perhaps too late and with too much of a shotgun approach.

Angels Without Snow Tires. Angels do not fear to tread in the inner city, but travel requires planning. One needs to be careful of the slippery streets of the secular city. Perhaps out of anger about its own guilt and shame over not being more active in urban and secular ministries, the Protestant bureaucracy rushed into secularism with little regard for its footing. Ministry is not simple or easy. The churches leaped to the scene so abruptly, however, that their witness seemed in retrospect to have introduced unusual theological, sociological, and political naïvete. Beware snowy streets without snow tires!

In a 1960 editorial *The Christian Century* declared: "When the secularists speak let the church listen."[15] The churches had failed. Now they must listen to the "children of darkness."

In a poignant essay Baptist pastor Warren Carr told of the integration crisis in his Southern town. Lay business leaders responded to massive racial demonstrations with the decision to integrate industry, school, hotel, motel, and food service. But they were fearful of the clergy issuing a statement or resolution. To Mr. Carr's feelings of impotency which this act had kindled, the town mayor responded: "'Don't discount the church,' he said. 'It has already done about all it can for us

---

[14]William Stringfellow, "Sin, Morality, and Poverty," *Christian Century* (June 2, 1965), pp. 703-6.

[15]"When the Secularists Speak Let the Church Listen," editorial, *Christian Century* (March 13, 1960), p. 308.

now. But if it hadn't been for the church I would never have been convinced that the Negro is morally right in this conflict.'"[16]

Church leaders were involved and wanted to be relevant, but the real secularists feared the inflamatory and inept political rhetoric of the clergy as secular politicians. Eager, by contrast, to get God's people out of the sanctuary and into the city, Gibson Winter decried the church as an institution (both parish and bureaucracy):

> The church will find its ministry of public responsibility through an apostolate of the laity and a ministry of servanthood in the structures of public life. This is her mission and opportunity in the emerging metropolis, but she cannot belong to this future and share in this ministry without the loss of her traditional structures and their false security.[17]

But the church in reality cannot have its witness both ways. Failing to appraise and appreciate fully the gains and losses of a drive into secularism, Harvey Cox's celebrated literary symbol *The Secular City* simply provided, as reviewer George Hall noted, a rationale for the bureaucracy to lurch down city streets. A subtle loss of nerve to be a theological or a secular entity yielded an insoluble dilemma. Cox's ambivalence was indeed the bureaucracy's ambivalence. Can or should one get along without theistic language and procedures in faith, believing only that God is the secular process? Some of the ambivalence was acted out by retaining God language, but the secular city was the major focus. God talk helped to generate revenue from suburbia and the small-town and rural hinterland. But the theological silence in the city was overwhelming. Cox thus provided a

---

[16]"Notes from an Irrelevant Clergyman," *Christian Century* (July 10, 1963), p. 880.

[17]Donald L. Benedict, "For a Reconciled Society," review of *The New Creation as Metropolis* by Gibson Winter, *Christian Century* (August 14, 1963), p. 1007.

legitimating linguistic touch allowing the churches to race off in at least two directions at once. Even the laity was purchasing *The Secular City!*

Soon revolutionary language entered the theological picture. God became a revolutionary but not without a sharp rebuttal. Sociologist Samuel Mueller notes:

> My point in discussing Cox's sources is to suggest that the most "relevant" churchmen are almost entirely out of touch with the academic discipline that has the most to say about the problems of man in the secular world. They simply have not been doing their sociological homework.[18]

Two specific implications are (1) *community organization:* "Persons of relatively high social status are much more likely to participate in voluntary organizations than are persons of relatively low social status" and (2) *administrative style:* "The tendency toward oligarchy has been noted in studies of other forms of voluntary organizations (*i.e.*, March of Dimes and American Baptist Convention). . . . similiar oligarchy tendencies can be observed in the mass action community organizations with which our relevant churchmen are so often identified."[19] Thus, the emphasis on life and action in the city (and not just talk) was not unambiguous or distinct in its life-style from the dead and dying institutional church.

Warnings about so-called Christian revolutionaries begin to find voice in the pages of *The Christian Century*. Editor Kyle Haselden reflected on the quagmire of an enlightened sadism that permeated the October 22-26, 1967, annual meeting of the National Council of Churches. The following program mood emerged:

> When violence aimed at systemic violence occurs it ought to be defended, supported and interpreted in such a manner as will aid,

---

[18]"Relevance, Community Organization, and Sociology," *Christian Century* (October 12, 1967) p. 1282.
[19]*Ibid.*, p. 1284.

hasten its end, and serve to establish a greater measure of justice.
. . . In any conflict between the government and the oppressed
. . . systemic violence [that of the church and other organizations]
may be violently confronted by its main victims as well as by
others on their behalf.[20]

Dr. Haselden concluded sadly, "More violence is undoubt-
edly on the way in this country. The church and the state are
by default of duty guaranteeing that calamity. But when
Christians preach the saving power of violence they, too,
contribute to the terror and evil of our time."

Robert Benne saw the need to establish limits on the use of
power:

> The exercise of power in the form of economic and political
> coercion seems less and less the answer to either our immediate
> or our long-range needs. The task that our society faces has
> shifted to another level. And the churches, instead of focusing on
> direct involvement in power, can best respond to the nation's
> problems by working on the level of what I shall call "cultural
> persuasion."[21]

Civil disobedience as a compelling action of conscience
requires community restraint as evidenced by Christopher
Lasch's commentary on the black power movement:

> It shares with the white left not only the language of romantic
> anarchism but several other features as well, none of them (it
> must be said) conducive to its success—a pronounced distrust of
> people over thirty, a sense of powerlessness and despair, for
> which the revolutionary rhetoric serves to compensate, and a
> tendency to substitute rhetoric for political analysis and defiant
> gestures for political action.[22]

---

[20] "Sense and Psychedelics," editorial, *Christian Century* (November 15,
1967), p. 1454.

[21] "The Limits of Power and the Need for Persuasion," *Christian Century*
(October 16, 1968), p. 1300.

[22] Christopher Lasch, *The Agony of the American Left*, reviewed by
William Hamilton, "The Left: Neither Gauche nor Sinister," *Christian
Century* (July 23, 1968), p. 995-96.

And finally, an annotated footnote on the bureaucratic carnage along the slippery streets of secularism was *The Christian Century* editorial on the ten-thousand-dollar gift from the United Presbyterian Church in the U.S.A., through COCAR, to the Angela Davis Defense Fund. Editor Geyer was encouraged: "Something very exciting has been happening in and around the UP Church these days . . . white Presbyterians have become freshly engaged in earnest wrestling over the essentials of Christian witness and racial justice."[23]

Despite Geyer's optimism the church leaders were not wise as foxes, innocent as doves. The bureaucracy had not yet come of age.

Whiplash: Resistance and Redemption. The preceding discussion pertained to the internal dynamics of the bureaucracy's uncritical overextension in the name of secular relevance. Accompanying this foray was a *theological whiplash*, more subtle and more painful than a reactionary backlash. The experience outside the formal bureaucracy was a profound disjointedness.

Many people and groups tried to relate positively to secularism. Now another fitful start and stop occurred, and a reaction of hurt, confusion, anger, but concerted response ensued. *The Christian Century* drew on Gibson Winter's *Suburban Captivity of the Churches* to identify some of the punches in this whiplash: (1) suburban churches are insular in a society that is urban and interdependent, (2) they are preoccupied with externals of a success cult (building and budget growth), and (3) they are engaged in an uncritical adaptation to culture.[24] This argument needed hearing, and

[23]"Angela and the Presbyterians," editorial, *Christian Century* (July 7, 1971), p. 823.
[24]"Submerged in Suburbia," editorial, *Christian Century* (March 22, 1961), p. 360-62.

54

some clergy responded, especially to the civil rights struggle and other social problems. The resultant tension between insular suburbia and social witness intensified, creating its own problems.

Aware of the almost schismatic cleavage which followed, Leroy Davis discussed the split between clergy and laity over involvement in social problems (the civil rights challenge most specifically), and in a curiously ambivalent way, he called for a new reformation in which primary attention should be to those who are of the household of faith.[25] His was a statesmanlike call for a strategic withdrawal to evaluate program without asking for a massive retreat. Perhaps too indirect and too veiled, it echoed a deep concern over the sundering of the oneness (clergy and laity) in the body of Christ. But following on the heels of the 1964 elections and the consensus for the war on poverty, for guns and butter, and for economic and political expansionism, it gave the national bureaucracies the signal for full speed ahead.

Concerned about the bureaucracy's use of social violence in its programs, William Biddle resisted open endorsement of revolution, arguing for evolution not revolution in *The Community Development Process*. His reviewer, Robert Lee, taunted this nostalgic, wistful, small-town hayseed with having urban action cold feet.[26] Perhaps. Lee punched at this resistance as "idealistic." Denying Biddle and Company any integrity, Lee gave the nonbureaucratic constituency another secular whiplash.

A fatal combination of intrinsic negativity and the psychological self-destructiveness of violence was becoming more apparent to many. But to a bureaucracy which

---

[25]"The Clergy-Laity Schism," *Christian Century* (November 25, 1964), p. 1456.

[26]"Idealistic Picture," review of *The Community Development Process* by William Biddle, *Christian Century* (June 29, 1966), p. 833.

continued to traffic in confrontation and revolutionary language, there appeared to be little danger. Roman Catholic theologian Rosemary Ruether summed it up: "So the disrupters end up with both a smashed head and a penalty for causing it." She saw one possible prescription for both backlash and whiplash in having a sense of humor to charm rather than shock. She did not want simply to drain off anger and outrage in innocent levity. But a balance between dead-pan grimness and redeeming laughter was needed to "get down to some really serious business."[27] Pursuing this line of conciliar mood toward serious business and perspective, Cynthia Wedel, president of the National Council of Churches, spoke to the whiplash issue. The leadership group had created a credibility gap with the average man and woman in the pew who still lived in another theological world. Dr. Wedel questioned whether arrogant and contemptuous leaders have made any real effort to reach the masses of church people with a clear, biblically based explanation of modern understanding of the church's mission.

> Church leaders who sincerely feel that the church must be more effective in influencing the moral climate and social patterns of our common life ought to realize that pressure on church members through statements and programs imposed from above may only heighten resistance and alienation. Careful analysis (some very good examples of which could be cited) may show that effort put into the education and involvement of a wide spectrum of church people at the local level can turn resisters into strong supporters. In a body like the church, where each individual *is* important, this is not only good strategy; it may be the only right way to act.[28]

But strategy and manipulation this was. This warm, sensitive, and sympathetic interest in the grass roots was not to hear or learn from the masses of the average man and

---

[27]"Confrontation and Communication," *Christian Century* (September 10, 1969), pp. 1163-65.

[28]"The Church and Social Action," *Christian Century* (August 12, 1970), p. 962.

woman, but to foster patience enough to change them. The assumption being that their resistance was a function of educational, theological, and cultural lag and did not have a judging and redeeming Word for the "leadership group" in the body of Christ. Tactically Wedel's gesture was sanguine and showed good sense. But the underlying issue ran more deeply than psychological resistance to the threat of novelty. The resistance may also have been the Word of redemption. As one of the more secure and sensitive professional bureaucrats, Dr. Wedel perceived the symptomatology correctly. Her perception, however, in the long run, may have induced a delayed whiplash and did not provide comfort for either grass roots or leaders.

Frontal and Flanking: Black Power, Feminists, and the New Evangelicals. The urge to the secular landscape was directed primarily toward a resolution of urban and civil rights problems. This activity was thorough, resourceful, and symbolically effective in demonstrating the gospel's relevance to these major issues. By the mid-sixties momentum was gathering in three other major areas of the church's life: the call for black awareness, the emergence of the feminists' perspective, and the growth of the conservative or evangelical spirit. These three areas posed a genuine threat to the bureaucracy in general. The earlier call to civil rights and civil cities was to a fairly unambiguous goal. Not everyone agreed what changes should be accomplished, but there was little open resistance among the denominations that some kind of improvement was needed. The bureaucrats mounting this integration and urban campaign were typically white, liberal, middle-class males. These folks were drawn primarily from the ranks of faithful servants in the church. But with blacks, women, and evangelicals pressing on the flanks and in a concerted frontal attack, bureaucrats were suddenly themselves the targets of criticism, and they discovered that

57

the demands for answers yielded no simple response. Most programatic efforts to respond either didn't work or were psychologically and sociologically—even theologically—unsatisfying to the three groups. The tension and rewards were raised to a high level of anxiety and conflict. Programs or funding to begin or aid programs represented only a partial satisfaction. The real goal or objective was becoming clear: Programs from the bureaucracy were not acceptable; to be the bureaucracy was fast becoming the goal. A piece of the action could no longer be a budget item entry, but to run the bureaucracy was where the action is.

Black Power. Whitney Young, executive director of the National Urban League acknowledged that "the churches turned the tide in winning passage of the Civil Rights bill." He did not want the churches to lose their momentum and moral commitment: "Either they help Negro citizens become constructive, productive consumers, or they condemn them to the status of chronic, destructive dependents reduced to making a career of welfare." Or—warfare! Not willing, or perhaps unable, to voice the imminence of black power, Malcolm X, and racial violence, Young was appealing to the old civil rights white liberals to close ranks with the Urban League. In retrospect this exhortation appeared as bland as a cocktail hour conversation barely hinting about what would soon happen.[29]

Be reminded that this article was published less than six months following the "long hot summer" of violence in Harlem. Eighteen months later a *Christian Century* editorial, "Black Power for Whom?" reflected this split in ideology and strategy within the civil rights movement between Southern Christian Leadership Conference, National Associ-

---

[29] "A Cry from the Dispossessed," *Christian Century* (December 9, 1964), pp. 1524-27.

ation for the Advancement of Colored People, and the Urban League in one camp; Congress on Racial Equality, SNCC, and the "black nationalist groups" in the other encampment. Said *The Christian Century*, "If CORE and SNCC now try to capture the whole civil rights movement they will be a graver threat to the Negro than to his white oppressor."[30]

Then came the full frontal attack: "Black Power" from Stokely Carmichael, *et al.* What a reversal and blow to the church bureaucrats who had been very active and successful in civil rights, especially in the sit-in movement beginning in 1960. A brief six years later both black and white were announcing failure.[31] Theologically this shift found initial expression among such people as Henry Mitchel who commented on the integrity and strength of black experience: "They [Malcolm X and Ron Karenga] would say that for the foreseeable future the black church has to be preserved as a base of Black Power. . . . If their identity [whites] or their motives are questioned [by blacks], they have to be as strong and creative as the black integratees have been all these years."[32] Put in more rhetorical tones, Gilbert Caldwell expressed the same conviction:

Every encounter with our white brother could provide us with an opportunity to minister, to emancipate, to liberate him. What new meaning might we now find in the many meetings we have to attend and be bored by! We have been bothered by the irrelevancy and duplicity, the "order without justice," the chicanery—but now instead of simply "losing our cool" or "telling whitey off" we should be able to see a new role for ourselves in this context. We could be involved in the process of humanizing

---

[30] "Black Power for Whom?" editorial, *Christian Century* (July 20, 1966), p. 903; "Put Down Your Buckets," editorial (August 3, 1966), p. 953.

[31] Margaret Halsey, "Integration Has Failed," *Christian Century* (December 28, 1966), pp. 1596-97.

[32] "Toward the 'New' Integration," *Christian Century* (June 12, 1968), p. 781.

and civilizing and sensitizing and converting our white colleagues.[33]

From essentially a liberal black perspective, others joined Caldwell in the flanking pressure: James Hunt, "Gandhi and The Black Revolution"; Preston Williams, "The Atlanta Document: An Interpretation"; Richard Soulen, "Black Worship and Hermeneutic."[34] Mounting the frontal assault against the white middle-class liberals was James Forman's Black Manifesto, issued and acted out in the spring of 1969.

Shocked, editor-at-large Howard Schomer claimed: "James Forman and Co. are not demanding one more set of reforms; they are sounding the tocsin of revolution. . . . The churches are but the first easy-access testing area for Forman's grand design."[35] The goals were no longer programs or reforms—but to be the bureaucracy, to storm the palace courtyard at 475 Riverside Drive. James Cone pressed the attack, "Black Power is an attempt to shape our present economic, social and political existence according to those actions that destroy the oppressor's hold on black flesh."[36] Blackness was an ontological symbol. "Black liberation is the new datum," claimed Cone. "It means adopting their [black] historical experience, realizing that we cannot be unless oppression ceases to be."[37] Ten years following the Greensboro sit-in Cone's radical theological statement about civil rights moved

[33]"Black Folks in White Churches," *Christian Century* (February 12, 1969), p. 210.

[34]Hunt, "Gandhi and the Black Revolution," *Christian Century* (October 1, 1969), pp. 1242-44; Williams, "Atlanta Document: An Interpretation," *Christian Century* (October 15, 1969), pp. 1311-12; Soulen, "Black Worship and Hermeneutic," *Christian Century* (February 11, 1970), p. 168.

[35]"The Manifesto and the Magnificat," editorial correspondence, *Christian Century* (June 25, 1969), p. 866.

[36]"Black Theology and Black Liberation," *Christian Century* (September 16, 1970), p. 1084.

[37]James Cone and William Hordern, "Dialogue on Black Theology," *Christian Century* (September 15, 1971), p. 1085.

from a far different perspective than that which motivated the bureaucrats in 1960 to close ranks with the sit-in movement.

The Feminist Perspective. In a brief but poignant article, "Women and the Church: Poor Psychology, Worse Theology," Sheila Collins (former seminary student, pastor's wife, and the mother of two preschool-age children) affirmed Betty Friedan's thesis in *The Feminine Mystique* that women suffer feelings of inadequacy, powerlessness, insecurity, and dependency; that, in other words, they have a poor self-image. Collins illustrated from a United Methodist church school curriculum task force related to the New York Annual Conference of The United Methodist Church. She reported some of the conclusions of that preliminary curriculum study:

> Yet absurd stereotypes of little girls are presented again and again in this curriculum. They would be laughable save for the fact that, like the image of the shuffling, bug-eyed Negro that was a convention in old movies, they play such a devastating role in the images little girls and boys begin to form of themselves.[38]

In a subtle and somewhat jesting article, Thomas Hearn looked at the other side of this coin and called for "male liberation." His was not so much an anger of being oppressed but an appreciative responsiveness to the feminist perspective: "For men need nothing less than a revolutionary new conception of what it is to be a man."[39]

In principle one might argue that the feminist perspective would have a positive impact among the bureaucracy. Generally those most supportive of Ms. Collins' concern were those in the soft disciplines such as psychology and

---

[38]"Women and the Church, Poor Psychology, Worse Theology," *Christian Century* (December 30, 1970), pp. 1557-58.

[39]"Jesus Was a Sissy After All," Readers' Response, *Christian Century* (October 7, 1970), p. 1192.

philosophy. Males in these areas may be expected to be supportive since their work involves a quality of passivity that deviates from the stereotype norm of the strong, self-reliant male. In a word, John Wayne would not picket for Hearn's male liberation because it complemented Collins. These liberators called for a revolutionary reorientation of male–female role models and blatant sex typology.

James Hitchcock, professor of history at St. Louis University, observed about the feminist thrust: "Its major theme that women have been wrongfully shut out from power and authority—even over their own lives—is essentially correct." But he worried over the rhetoric and method, and the theological implications pertaining to the changes:

> My basic objection to certain aspects of women's lib is again that they smack of idolatry. When the NCRWTE report says that women's liberation is "not just another revolution among others," and predicts that it will totally transform society, I think it comes close to being idolatrous.[40]

This degree of militancy, this reversal of roles and exposure of oppressive and debilitating prejudices, would catch the average, well-meaning, middle-class white male quite off guard. How would a white male respond to this? By 1971 surely the church bureaucracy was expressing ethnic pluralism and, therefore, black general church executives co-opted or would tend to form a coalition with the women partly due to similar oppressive experiences and partly to gain reinforcements in their frontal attack, and to prevent the women from outflanking the black males in their quest to be the bureaucracy.

Relevancy was being shifted rapidly from programs to "being itself." *Being the bureaucracy* was enough—that, plus a healthy travel and entertainment budget. The tasks and

---

[40]"Women's Liberation: Tending Toward Idolatry," *Christian Century* (September 22, 1971), p. 1107.

functions that the bureaucracy is to perform for the church-in-general were either being curtailed or done less effectively or not at all. They were a smoke screen or down payment on the "rent" so that the hallways, offices, banquet rooms, and airplane seats could be occupied—and reversal of roles and oppression continue!

The New Evangelicals. The first wind of this came with the Jesus movement when suddenly a secular society began to pay attention (in a distrustful and bemused fashion) to those wanting to be known as Jesus People. Many of these persons were cultural and drug dropouts. But interestingly the word *Jesus* enjoyed a new respectibility and vocabulary currency that transcended a fundamentalist stereotype of the poor, rural agarian whites and blacks. From the opening volley by the Children of God and other Jesus communes, the theological climate began to change. In a review of Max Stackhouse's publication of Walter Rauschenbusch's *Righteousness of the Gospel,* Paul Preachy noted: "Nonetheless the work has a contemporary ring, particularly in respect to the need to change 'structures.' But in contrast to current intoners Rauschenbusch never forgets his evangelical roots."[41]

A month later Paul Holmer reviewed Donald Bloesch's *Crisis of Piety* and observed:

> Instead of relating modern theological themes to action, to policy issues and to a preoccupation with the secular world, Professor Bloesch uses Bonhoeffer and the others to bring us back to personal matters and questions about the health of the human spirit.[42]

---

[41] "Early Social Gospel," review of *The Righteousness of the Kingdom* by Walter Rauschenbusch, *Christian Century* (October 2, 1968), p. 1245.

[42] "Pro Piety," review of *The Crisis of Piety: Essays Toward a Theology of the Christian Life* by Donald Bloesch, *Christian Century* (November 6, 1968), p. 1407.

More flanking than frontal, the new Evangelicals were unburying themselves from the eclipse of a vital, strong, socially sensitive piety. Partly the Jesus People helped; partly new intellectual blood helped (Bloesch, Schaeffer, Montgomery, *et al.*); partly the charismatic movement; partly the World Conference on Evangelism (The Frankfurt Declaration, 1970). Perhaps the single most significant catalyst was the strong affirmation that the kingdom of God was not coterminous with the destiny of the United States. Dropped into the midst of the nationalist ambiguity of American manifest destiny dislodged by the urban riots, assassinations, the peace movement, the Berrigans, the national political party nominating conventions (especially 1968 and 1972), and the early scent of Watergate, this theological perspective provided a new ideological cohesiveness. Symbolized most directly by the *Post-American* magazine, it was expressed in *The Christian Century* by Richard Mouw:

> On October 11, 1972, 50 evangelicals representing many congregations, colleges and seminaries, and organizations such as Youth for Christ, Young Life and Inter-Varsity Christian Fellowship, held a breakfast meeting with George McGovern in a Chicago suburb. Later in the morning black evangelist Tom Skinner spoke the mind of most of that gathering when he introduced George McGovern at Wheaton (Illinois) College with an enthusiastic endorsement of McGovern's candidacy.
>
> That the McGovern breakfast took place ten years to the day from the opening of the Second Vatican Council is of no importance save as it served to lend point to the fact that American evangelicalism is experiencing a show of political aggiornamento, of which the breakfast meeting and the larger "Evangelicals for McGovern" organization, as well as the "radical evangelicalism" of the recently formed Peoples Christian Coalition, are significant expressions.[43]

---

[43]"Evangelicals and Political Activism," *Christian Century* (December 27, 1972), p. 1316.

This change, plus a conference held in Grand Rapids, Michigan, April 13-14, 1973, and reported by *The Christian Century* under the title, "In Search of a Theology of Politics":

Another instance was the charge by the political evangelical *Post-American's* Jim Wallis that mainline evangelicalism accepts a "naïve theological liberalism" which "fails to see the effects of sin on our *national* life." Insisting that the conference had engaged in "too much talk about politics and not enough about discipleship," he argued that America's problems are "theological, not political." Wallis exhorted evangelicals to develop a life style of "resistance" appropriate to a "biblical people"—one rooted in scriptural teaching and sustained by a life of prayer.[44]

This was followed in November, 1973, by an evangelical ecumenical statement on social concerns called the "Chicago Declaration" or "Declaration of Evangelical Social Concern." Here were new stirrings and a new power base from old ashes.

Much of the frontal-attack rhetoric directed toward the denominational bureaucracy reflected the themes of oppressed people gracefully articulated by black theologian James Cone and by white Roman Catholic theologian Peggy Way. Here were the making of an oppressed people's coalition. The new Evangelicals could not hitch their wagon to that political star. But three factors made the new Evangelicals a serious threat to the bureaucracy: (1) The mood of the times was more conservative and serious reassessment of basic questions (population, fossil fuels, pollution, church membership decline, etc.) were coming out as theological issues and lending credence to the raising of doctrinal matters; (2) Evangelicals generally had been supportive of church programs, but they were becoming "critically supportive" of the denomination, and (3) a warm

---

[44] Mouw, "In Search of a Theology of Politics," *Christian Century* (May 2, 1973), p. 502.

affirmation of Donald Bloesch's call for a new piety, a health of the spirit, was abroad in the land. The coalescing of these factors fell outside the personal theological comfortability range of most bureaucrats. The evangelical action was more flanking than frontal. But once again the bureaucrats were being pressed by a significant group of people to whom they did not have primary allegiance.

These three diverse but organizationally similar groups were not going to go away in the near future. The test case now is, How effectively can the bureaucracy relate to the blacks, women, and new Evangelicals and still continue to carry on their perceived mission and the mandates given by their parent organization, the denomination. This forecasts a difficult period ahead.

PART 2
The Religious Bureaucratic System

Chapter 4
Becoming a Bureaucrat

The persons who manage the national church agencies are the professional staff. The board of directors determines the policies of the agency. The staff carry out these policies and are responsible for the day-to-day operations. The contact that the pastor has with an agency is usually with a staff member.

These persons, like the organizations for which they work, are frequently misunderstood by their constituents. Many people are unclear concerning what the bureaucrat does. One long-term staff member described himself as having the kind of job that makes it difficult to explain to his wife's relatives what he does for a living.

The lay and clergy professional staff of the national Protestant agencies as a group are alert, intelligent, hardworking, and dedicated church persons. Many give themselves to their task with a religious zeal. They are also uptight, insecure, and uncertain about the future of the organization for which they work and their place in it. More persons are actively seeking other employment than at any other time in the recent history of American Protestantism. Probably more professional staff members have lost their jobs since 1970 than in any other comparable time span. Replacements are increasingly hard to hire.

This chapter will focus on the bureaucrats who manage the national agencies. It will deal with the selection of staff, their career possibilities, what happens when threatened with dismissal, and the relationship between the board and staff and the lay person in the bureaucracy.

Who Gets Hired

Church agencies differ in how persons are selected for staff positions. In some agencies a search or personnel committee seeks the best person for the job. Some positions may be filled by the chief executive with the approval of the board. In some organizations board members take an active part in all hiring; in others they only choose the higher-echelon personnel. But the process of staff selection and the types of persons hired has been changing.

In the past the national agencies tended to hire staff members from among people who were doing similar tasks in the regional judicatories. Thus for a position in the field of new church development, a national agency would tend to invite a regional executive who had successfully supervised the establishment of several new congregations or a pastor who had built several new churches. A person to supervise the national program of urban ministries would tend to be someone who had demonstrated ability in a similar task in a major metropolitan area. Executives for the overseas missionary enterprise were selected from among the most successful missionaries. Persons employed to direct the denomination's educational work were recruited from those working in related fields in the judicatories or local churches.

There were some exceptions to this pattern of staff recruitment. Certain positions require technical expertise in such fields as audio-visuals or research. In these cases individuals with the required technical training were sought.

Even here persons employed elsewhere in the denomination were often found.

A national agency is always in danger of having a regional executive try to find a job for someone who must move from his present post. A staff position is a convenient way of kicking an individual upstairs. This may solve a local personnel problem by "promoting" the individual in question to a job at a national level.

In one instance a regional executive needed to help a pastor relocate. In order to have a church available for this individual he prevailed upon a national agency to hire a particular pastor, thus creating the desired vacancy. The agency executive employed the individual and assigned him to a department. The department head was on vacation when these events, which took only a couple weeks, occurred. Upon his return he was surprised, and not particularly overjoyed, to learn that he had an unexpected subordinate.

It should be noted that not all of the persons whom the national agencies are pressured to employ are problems. Some are individuals whose particular skills can be better utilized in a bureaucratic job than as pastor of a local church. Many regional executives simply will not transfer their personnel problems to the national bureaucracy.

Another source of staff, particularly at the higher levels, are persons who are members of the board of directors. They tend to have acquired some knowledge of the operation of the agency and may be natural candidates for an executive position. They are known to the chief executive and the other board members who make the selection. Furthermore, they have participated in the formulation of the agency's policies. By hiring one of its own, a board can be reasonably sure that its policies will be carried out.

The long-established practice of selecting professional staff from among the persons employed by the regional judicatories and from among the board members has been changing. There are two parts to the current trend. The first has been to hire persons who are not employed in similar posts in the regional judicatory and often with no experience in a similar job. This has tended to bring to the staff somewhat younger persons, often with more academic training but less experience. It also brought persons who have a different perspective on what the agencies should be doing and how they relate to their constituency.

The second trend has been to employ more women and persons representing ethnic and cultural groups. Some agencies have adopted a quota system requiring a proportion of positions be filled by women and minority persons. The implications of this change are discussed in detail in a subsequent chapter.

The process by which potential staff persons are discovered has been changing. Instead of the agency seeking someone to fill a vacancy, positions are being advertised so any interested party may apply. It is not certain as yet whether this procedure will make any difference in the long run. In the final analysis an informal selection process may still prevail. An agency may advertise a position but still hire someone who is a board member or the candidate of the top executive.

The evidence is that even when a position is advertised, the agencies are not deluged with applications. One organization advertised for applications to fill a coming vacancy in its top executive post; yet, only fourteen applications were received for one of the most important jobs in that denomination.

Staff Mobility

The cleric who accepts a position as a staff member in the national church bureaucracy may feel that he or she is moving "up" in the denomination. He may see himself as having nationwide (or at least denomination-wide) responsibility and exerting wide influence. Usually he receives a raise in salary. His peers tend to share his perception of the new job, seeing it as having higher status than the pastor of a local church or a staff member of a regional judicatory.

In the excitment of moving into a national office, the individual may not seriously consider where his new position can lead. He may feel that he has arrived at the pinnacle of his career. It is not surprising that a new staff member fails to realize that he may have accepted a dead-end job. Some agency executives, particularly in the recent period of personnel reductions, have been shocked to learn that they literally had no place within the church to go when facing dismissal.

There are two axioms that apply to the individual who wishes to or must leave the employment of the bureaucracy. The first is that the difficulty in finding another job elsewhere in the church increases with the length of time that the individual has been on the staff. The second is that the difficulty in finding a comparable position increases in proportion to the level one has attained in the bureaucracy. A top executive may find it harder to secure satisfactory employment elsewhere in the church than one of his subordinates.

The person who prior to his employment in the bureaucracy had only training for and experience in the pastorate may find himself in a particularly awkward situation. The experience and skills he developed while with a national agency do not prepare him to return to the local church. These skills are not what pulpit committees usually seek. The bureaucrat has not been preaching regularly nor counseling with individuals. A congregation may be reluctant to call or a bishop to appoint someone who has been away from the pastoral ministry for a long period of time. Accepting a parish

71

is virtually a mid-career change of occupations for the agency employee. The cleric is in quite a different position than the attorney who has served with a federal agency. The lawyer may find that the expertise and contacts acquired in Washington are considered assets by law firms. The minister seeking to return to the pastorate may find that his years of service in the church bureaucracy are a liability.

The high-level staff executive has particular difficulty. Positions with comparable salary and status are not available in the church. The higher one's position in the church bureaucracy, the more difficult it is to leave without seeming to have been demoted. This explains in part why board executives develop a strong vested interest in their position. With no place to go, they may hang on tenaciously.

The situation is further complicated by the sense of vocation that the pastor brings to his job. He sees his work for the national agency as an expression of his ministry. Indeed, the church expects its clergy to make a life-long commitment to the ministry. A candidate for admission into a United Methodist annual conference is asked, "Are you resolved to devote yourself wholly to God and his work?" Some staff members who have lost their positions have felt that the church did not keep faith with them. They see themselves as having been faithful but now being rejected by the institution that expected and received their commitment.

Despite the fact that the pastor's experience as a national staff member might lead to a variety of positions outside of the church, to accept one may seem to be a repudiation of his ministerial calling. The result is that the individual may remain in an agency position when those directly involved know it would be better for him and the organization to terminate the relationship.

If the individual is willing to seek employment outside the church, he can frequently secure a responsible position at a comparable or better salary. One church executive who lost his position because of a drastic reduction in funds easily secured an important administrative post with a secular agency. As an ordained clergyman he left the church employ with reluctance, despite the fact that his denomination could not find a parish for him. Another minister, who was forced to leave a national agency due to a reorganization, was unable to locate a parish at half his salary. He finally became vice-president of a savings and loan association.

There are of course exceptions to the rule that a staff position is a dead-end job. A few individuals have been elected bishop or moved to different parts of the bureaucracy. Others have accepted administrative positions in denominational institutions such as colleges or retirement homes. Some with appropriate academic credentials have become seminary or college professors. These persons have been exceptions rather than the rule.

Upward mobility within the agencies tends to be restricted. The chances that the staff member will rise from the lower echelons to an executive position are slim. The trend has been to bring persons into the bureaucracy from the outside, particularly to fill the higher positions. There are two reasons for this. The first is the patronage system in the denominations that rewards significant persons, including women and minorities, with executive posts. The second is the general distrust of the national staff members, a phenomenon that places them at a distinct disadvantage when openings occur.

Procedures for Termination

There is no good way to terminate an employee; it is a traumatic experience. The combination of restructure and decrease in income has required the dismissals during the past several years of a large number of staff members. The church agencies have handled separations in different ways. Their procedures have ranged from commendable to shameful.

Those agencies which discharged a large number of staff at approximately the same time devised a policy that provided certain benefits to those leaving. The United Presbyterian Church in the U.S.A. gave its employees job-hunting time, paid for career-counseling services up to four hundred dollars, provided for 50 percent of an employment agency's fee, paid for 50 percent of interview expenses up to six hundred dollars, authorized retraining costs up to six hundred dollars, and gave severance pay ranging from two weeks' salary for those employed less than one year to twenty-six weeks salary for persons who had worked twenty-four years or longer.[1]

As of June 30, 1973, all positions in the bureaucracy of the United Presbyterian Church in the U.S.A. ceased to exist. Individuals could apply for their job (if it was to exist in the new structure) or for any other job. Other persons were invited to apply. The new organization was staffed by some persons who were retained and by some who were newly hired. By erasing the slate, the agencies were able to eliminate certain staff members simply by not rehiring them. This procedure had a devastating effect on morale. Some persons felt that it was an indignity to be asked to reapply for a position they held and had been performing satisfactorily. The persons who were terminated possibly could feel that their job was eliminated through forces beyond their control rather than their performance. It is hard to imagine a procedure which could have produced a greater degree of staff anxiety and hostility over a fairly long period of time.

The Episcopal Church moved quickly when it became

---

[1] "Transitional Personnel Policies for General Assembly Board and Agency Personnel of the United Presbyterian Church in the United States of America," duplicated paper (April 21, 1972).

necessary to reduce staff. A drastic decrease in income in 1970 required that a large number of employees had to be discharged. The senior executives, with the advice of a small group of staff and an outside management consultant, decided which persons would go. The decisions were made within ten days. Persons being terminated were notified by December 31, 1970, that their employment would end March 31, 1971. Benefits included four days' termination pay for every year of service, career counseling, and up to three hundred dollars for retraining.[2]

When the Presbyterian Church in the U.S. reduced its number of employees, severance pay was provided in proportion to their length of service. The agency executives attempted to assist staff members find other positions somewhere within the church. The relatively small size of the denomination and the effectiveness of the informal system of communication made this possible, and employment was found for most persons. While some individuals were hurt, those responsible are convinced that the procedure was as humane and considerate as possible.

The United Methodist bureaucracy did not have to terminate a large number of employees at a given time. There were a number of staff discharged as new boards and new executives sought persons with different skills and attitudes. The denomination did not develop an overall formal policy for severance pay and career consulting, but left the matter to each agency.

The United Methodist minister who is a member of an annual conference is guaranteed an appointment. Thus the ordained bureaucrat who loses his job can in theory return to his annual conference and be reappointed as a pastor of a congregation. In actual practice a variety of factors influence

---

[2] "Reorganization of the Executive Council Staff," duplicated paper (December 8, 1970).

the bureaucrat's ability to return to the pastorate, including the individual's skill and interests and the availability of churches in an annual conference when he wishes an appointment. Most persons terminated by United Methodist agencies were given sufficient notice so that they secured other positions on their own initiative.

There are a number of instances of employees being treated in a most inhumane manner. One case will illustrate. A senior staff member, fifty-four years old who holds an earned doctorate, was in his tenth year of service. In January, 1975, he heard rumors from several secretaries that he was to be discharged. He did not take these seriously because earlier that month he had received a letter signed by two senior executives informing him of his reappointment for the year 1975, announcing that he would receive a substantial raise in salary effective January 1, and thanking him for his valuable service. When the rumors persisted, he went to his immediate superior on January 30 and asked if they were true. He was then told that the personnel committee of the agency had decided at a meeting held the preceding October to terminate him, but they had given the executive the option of determining when and in what manner the decision was to be implemented. The staff member was told that he should secure another position. He received no response to the obvious question of why he was being fired. A subsequent meeting with the chief executive of the agency and an interview with the personnel committee produced no rationale for his dismissal.

It was soon learned that a replacement had been hired. This was an Asian-American pastor who was a member of the board of directors and chairman of the board committee which had the responsibility of supervising the discharged person's work. Thus the board of directors had dismissed a staff member and replaced him with a member of their own group.

The terminated staff member maintained a sense of dignity but felt keenly the injustice and humiliation to which he had been subjected. He stated that he had informed the executive of the agency some two years earlier that if he ever wanted to replace him with a member of a minority group, he would resign to make this possible. He also stated that if he had been privately asked to resign, he would have made every effort to secure another position and leave quietly. Having been fired, he left under a cloud and without understanding the specific reasons for his dismissal.

Overall, church agencies do not receive high marks for their termination procedures. A leading United Presbyterian commented, "We would not do business with a company that treated their employees the way our church has treated its staff." A United Methodist bishop wrote, "One other matter that is of major concern to me is the fact that we have apparently considered general church personnel expendable on the altar of restructure."

It is impossible to avoid the impression that some persons responsible for the administration of church agencies find it difficult to make and implement a decision about the individual's performance. There is ample evidence that in many cases there is a lack of forthrightness and honesty in dealing with individuals. The result is that staff members are needlessly injured both personally and professionally.

The Lay Person in the Church Bureaucracy

A majority of the staff members in the national Protestant agencies are ordained clergy. The reason for this is twofold. First, many of the positions require ordination not necessarily for the actual work involved, but because of the relationship which the staff member has with a largely ministerial constituency. The type of leadership expected from the national church agencies probably would not be possible without a substantial proportion of the professional staff being ordained. The clergy who have most direct contact with the bureaucracy expect that a substantial proportion of staff will be ordained. One United Methodist bureaucrat reported that as he travels around the country he is frequently asked if he is a clergy or lay. The question is not put directly. Rather a minister will want to know, "Of what annual conference are you a member?" This is simply a subtle way of finding out whether the staff member is a minister or a lay person.

A second reason for the employment of a large number of clergy is that they are more likely to know about available agency positions. They see such jobs as a further development of their career. For the lay person to go to work for the church may mean a drastic career change, including a salary reduction. The possibility of returning to secular employment is uncertain. One denominational executive was a successful architect who sold his practice to accept a position with a church agency. Should he desire to return to architecture he would have to begin to develop his practice and clientele anew. While the same thing may be true for some of the clergy staff members, they do not seem to be as keenly aware of it as the lay employees.

The church bureaucracy has always had a number of lay persons on the staff, some for long periods of time. Some lay employees have specialized skills in finance, legal counsel, architecture, and so forth. Others occupy a wide range of administrative positions throughout the church agencies.

The lay employees tend to be indistinguishable from clergy in similar positions. The lay person in an executive position does not appear to perform differently from the minister in a similar job. In fact, many lay employees are career church bureaucrats. Some are recruited from similar jobs in the regional judicatories. Thus a treasurer in a regional office may be offered a similar job by a national agency. A business manager of a larger congregation becomes the head of the denomination's central treasury. A director of Christian education in a local church is employed by the national educational agency. A large proportion of the lay persons employed by the national church agencies are actually unordained religious professionals who see their careers as being within the denomination.

A lay employee faces a somewhat different situation than a cleric when he loses his position with a church agency. The pastor is assumed to have the option of again becoming a parish minister (assuming that he can receive a call or is willing to accept the church to which the bishop will appoint him). The opportunities for the lay person to secure comparable employment will depend on a number of factors such as the individual's particular skills, age, willingness to relocate, and the job market at the time.

The number of lay employees will probably increase. The pressure by the organized women's group to hire more women will be the chief reason for this. While a few of those employed will be ordained, the vast majority will be lay persons. The growing number of blacks and other ethnic minorities being employed will also contribute to the increase in lay staff. Nevertheless, a large proportion of blacks and ethnics are and probably will continue to be ordained clergy.

When an individual accepts a position as a staff member in a national agency, he or she embarks on a career different from that of most religious workers. The next chapter will examine some aspects of life in the Protestant bureaucracy.

Chapter 5
The View of and from the National Office

The offices of churches' agencies look much like those of insurance companies, government bureaus, and a thousand other organizations. Like many of their secular counterparts, most occupy new buildings, an indication of the affluent self-image of the Protestant denominations in the 1950s and 1960s. If one looks closely it is possible to note some subtle differences between the offices of church and secular agencies. Some Christian symbol will be found in the church offices, not prominently displayed but clearly in evidence. It may be a sculpture or a wood carving in the elevator lobby or on the wall near the receptionist's desk. Somewhere in the building there is usually a chapel, a room valued more for its symbolic expression than actual use.

In the private office of the church agency executive are the typical tools of the middle manager. There is a telephone with several buttons, dictating equipment, file cabinets, and a bookcase with the agency's annual reports for as many years as the individual has been a member of the staff. If the person is a senior executive the office will have a conference table for committee meetings. Somewhere will be at least one Christian symbol, often a cross hanging on the wall or one standing upright on the bookcase or desk. One pauses to wonder what the children in a confirmation class from a nearby church may think as their pastor brings them on a tour of the agency headquarters.

The church bureaucrat lives in a world of correspondence and committees, memos and meetings. Although part of the church, the day-to-day work bears little resemblance to the sermons, study, counseling, and the close relationships that a pastor has with people in a parish. The actual work of the bureaucrat may be more like that of the insurance company or bank across the street. Is the agency employee a spiritual leader or simply a manager? How does he see himself and how is he seen by the clergy and laity of his denomination?

Ambiguous describes how the church bureaucrat is seen by his constituents and how he perceives himself. Among the clergy there is always some degree of antagonism toward the general agencies. At the same time a national staff position is viewed as one of high status, more important than that of the average parish minister. Some of the resentment directed at the bureaucrat may be an expression of envy.

The staff member soon becomes aware that both the clergy and lay people regard him as a person of importance. His counsel is often sought, especially if his responsibilities include the granting of funds. By definition he is the "expert" from the national office. Unless he is very young, he may be addressed as "Doctor" even if he holds no such degree. The individual may have accepted a national agency staff position with the motivation to serve the church and be aware of his personal limitations and a little uncomfortable by the status he is accorded.

Thus the church bureaucrat finds himself in a position that is seen as having high prestige but is also the object of resentment. He may approach his task with humility while continually being reminded that he is one of his denomination's influential leaders. These forces help shape the way he perceives the world from the national office.

The Clergy as Bureaucrat

Many professional staff persons employed by the national church agencies are ordained clergy. Some were selected for their positions because they were prominent ministers with an interest in the work of the agency, possibly having been a member of the board of directors. What kind of bureaucrat is the cleric with his particular outlook and training likely to become?

If a person is wanted who will fit smoothly into the organization, live by the rules without complaint, and work quietly to provide services to the constituency, the cleric is an inappropriate person to hire. Ministers as a group usually want to change things and get people to undertake specific activities. The desired changes may range from persuading the individual to forsake his sinful ways to reorganizing the society. When pastor of a local church, the bureaucrat had the responsibility of seeing that people in his congregation got things done, ranging from running the Sunday school to organizing the annual finance campaign. He continually recruited persons for activities from singing in the choir to painting the fellowship hall. Promoting programs was his stock in trade, programs to educate his people and persuade them to act.

When such a person accepts a position with a national church agency what happens to his style of work? He still wants to get things accomplished, but he does not have the members of a congregation with whom to work. His energies are devoted to designing programs for all the congregations or all the people. The denomination becomes his parish, and it receives his enthusiastic attention.

One of the traits of a minister is to organize a parish "in his own image." A new pastor often changes many of the procedures of his predecessor. He brings his own operating style and program emphases to the congregation. The

82

preacher turned bureaucrat will tend not to be content with following established procedures and programs, but he will want to do things his own way.

A new chief executive frequently makes physical changes in the arrangement of the offices. One man had several partitions relocated in order to move his office about forty feet from the corner to the center of the building. Another had a new entrance to the building constructed. These expensive alterations contribute little to the primary task of the organization. They are a symbol that a new administration has taken over and that changes are being made.

By employing large numbers of clergy whose training and experience have been in the organization and promotion of programs, an active bureaucracy is assured.

A Sense of Elitism

A danger lurks in the energy and ability inherent in the staff of the national Protestant agencies. Some come to view themselves as an elite leadership corps whose task is to provide direction for the denomination. As members of the knowledgeable elite they are confident of the direction the church should take. As activitists they are prepared to work to move their church in the proper course.

The staff members' role in designing and administering programs tends to reinforce the idea that they are an elite leadership group. They prepare the proposals that are then brought to the boards of directors for their consideration and approval or disapproval. The final decisions concerning programs to be adopted and funds to be allocated are made by the board of directors. It is the professional staff, however, who do much of the work and have great personal interest in the success of the agency's programs.

Another factor contributing to the sense of elitism is the

use of national church agencies to further some causes opposed by certain segments within the constituency. This is done with the support of the denominational leaders or at least a strong majority of them. The professional staff members must favor such action as they are the persons who will provide the direct leadership. The best examples were the participation of national church agencies in the civil rights movement in the Deep South in the 1960s. Church funds were contributed and staff members worked in the civil rights campaigns despite strong opposition by many church people and leaders in the Southern churches. The use of national church agencies to work for causes opposed by some parts of the church reinforces the idea that the judgments of persons in the national offices are superior, making the agency staff a kind of theological Green Beret corps.

A major factor helping to create a sense of elitism in the church agencies is the isolation of the staff from the constituency. The bureaucrats talk most frequently with each other. The day-to-day contact with colleagues is far greater than that with persons in the churches across the nation. The staff person's view of the denomination tends to be influenced by persons more like himself than by the rank and file clergy and church members.

Staff of larger organizations spend a large amount of time with each other. There are more possibilities for committees and the perceived need for coordinating activities. One executive reported that when he had a board of directors of 32 people and a staff of 10, he spent 80 percent of his time working in his professional field and 20 percent in administration. The restructure resulted in a merger of his agency into one with a board of managers of 125 persons. As part of this larger organization, he reported that the proportions of his time were reversed. He was spending 80 percent of his time on administration, having to attend more meetings and "working to protect my flanks." A sense of elitism results

84

from staff members spending a large amount of time with each other.

The professional staff members see themselves as the persons who provide leadership to enable the church to break through into new areas or in the once popular jargon, to be the "cutting edge" of the denomination. This contributes to an attitude that perceives persons in the local congregations as provincial in their thinking and attitudes, incapable of providing the fresh new ideas for the church. The result is an unhealthy relationship between the agencies and those whom they are supposed to serve. The bureaucrat feels superior to his constituency, and the rank and file resent the national agencies.

Two factors prevent the relationship between bureaucracy and clientele from being worse. The first is the minority of staff members who somehow do not feel superior to the clergy and people in the local churches. The second is the limited contacts that the national staff have with persons at the grass roots. Many people are blissfully unaware of the elitist attitudes.

Symbols of Office

The symbols of rank within the church agency contribute to the individual's sense of importance. They indicate one's position within the organization. The size of office, the style of furniture, and whether there is or is not carpet will depend on the person's rank. In one agency the salary of the secretary depended on the rank of the professional staff person. Thus the lower-echelon staff members were assured of either the inexperienced or less competent secretaries. The secretary in turn had to move to a higher ranking person in order to receive a promotion and raise in salary.

Titles are important because they signify the individual's

status within the organization and denote the salary level. Therefore it is significant to the bureaucrat whether he or she is executive secretary, director, executive director, general secretary, associate general secretary, assistant general secretary, or field staff.

The symbols of office and titles are taken with great seriousness by church bureaucrats, as they are by bureaucrats everywhere. The writer once stopped in to see a person employed in a church agency. In the course of the conversation he inquired where the unit that this individual headed fitted into the larger organization. The response was, "We are a bureau, but we have the status of an office," an important if unclear distinction.

The emphasis on the trappings of office is probably inevitable considering the sinful nature of man and the complexities of human organizations. Nevertheless, it does contribute to the separation of the church bureaucrat from his constituency by reinforcing the idea that the agency is of primary importance.

The bureaucrat may come to think that the average pastor or lay person has an equally high interest in and regard for the symbols of office. Actually most people are interested in whether the agency is performing its task effectively and not in such matters as its internal organization or the status of its executives. An example of the worst kind of bureaucratic thinking was a three-page promotional brochure produced by a mission agency. It contains a picture of the nineteen-story Interchurch Center, the New York office building which probably contains the largest number of Protestant bureaucrats in the world to be found under one roof. The text read in part:

Window to the National Division. It looks like a lot more than that to me. Well it really is a lot more . . . almost all the ones on the third floor.

86

Don't you wish we could jump right up and look in the windows and see all those great big New York executives at work?[1]

The church members who contribute to missions know there must be administrators and overhead, but they hope both will be kept to a minimum. They are not likely to be positively impressed by having the fact that the third floor is out of touch—and out of reach—called to their attention.

The Chief Executive

The style of a national church agency is to a large degree determined by the chief executive. This is the top administrator of an agency or of a major division of a large agency. His or her influence on the organization is far greater than is often realized. It is exerted in several crucial areas.

First, the chief executive is the individual through whom the board of directors relates to the rest of the staff. Proposals from the staff that require the approval of the board of directors go through the top executive. He is in a position to encourage certain courses of action and discourage or even veto others. His influence on the activities of an agency can be decisive.

Second, the chief executive may determine who is hired. Even when the board of directors makes the actual final selection, the executive may select two or three candidates for the job. The board may then choose one for the position. Even if he cannot select a new staff member, he may be able to veto an unacceptable candidate. If an executive remains in the post for a long enough time, he can remake the agency by the kind of people he secures for his staff.

Third, the top administrator will greatly influence the

---

[1]*Window to the National Division* (New York: Board of Global Ministries, The United Methodist Church, 1974).

course of the agency by how he relates to his staff members. He controls staff assignments, salary increases, and promotions. Thus his goals for the agency will be translated in the decisions he makes concerning what assignments the staff members are given. Persons who can meet the executive's expectations will receive promotions.

When a board of directors wants to make major changes in an organization, they first must replace the chief executive with someone whose understanding coincides with theirs. A new administrator also must be able to replace a sufficient number of staff to ensure that there is adequate consensus to enable the agency to move in the desired direction.

Tension Between the Bureaucracy and Its Constituency

Tension between the bureaucracy and its constituency is caused by several factors. One is the inertia or resistance by the constituency to do what the bureaucrats want them to do. The volume of mail about which pastors so often complain usually brings requests that their congregations do something such as study a specific topic or contribute to some cause. The objection to the mail is really resistance to the requests that the letters bring.

Money is a major cause of tension. The bureaucracy is in constant need of more funds. There have never been and never will be adequate financial resources to support the spiritual and human needs with which the national church agencies are concerned. Hence the bureaucracy maintains constant pressure on their constitutency to contribute more money. Bureaucrats believe that the average church member can and should contribute more money to the causes promoted and administered by the agencies; but the clergy and lay people are not convinced of this.

No one likes to have taxes raised, even those that are voluntary. Thus the constant pressure to increase contributions or to divert funds from use in the congregation or local community to the denominational programs is a continual source of tension. This does not generally develop into open conflict because church members believe in most of the things the agencies are doing.

The greatest tension between the bureaucracy and the constituency occurs when an agency supports a cause that is strongly opposed by a large number of people. The causes of such tension arouse strong emotions and receive wide publicity. The particular subject of the controversy will vary. It often is a matter related to the action of an agency on a particular social issue, although conflict may also be over a theological difference. The ten-thousand-dollar contribution by a United Presbyterian agency to the defense fund for Angela Davis was violently opposed by many people and resulted in a serious decline in income. The feelings were so strong and the reaction so intense it caused an official to comment, "The new structure will assure that we [the United Presbyterian Church in the U.S.A.] will never have an Angela Davis incident again."

A source of tension within The United Methodist Church is the theology of foreign missions and its effect on the number of American missionaries overseas. The unresolved conflict is between the evangelical wing of the denomination and the denomination's foreign mission agency. Each group has a different understanding of the purpose of overseas missions. Compromise between the two groups has proved impossible. After a year and one-half of formal negotiations, meetings between the two groups were suspended. The theological assumptions of each were so far apart that a middle position acceptable to both sides has been impossible to attain.

The reorganization of the national church agencies has probably increased the tension between the bureaucracy and its constituency. It has resulted in the employment of many new staff members. These persons want to make their contribution, which means new program emphases and activities. These require new funds or the shifting of money from existing programs. Tension occurs in both cases, either in the resistance to requests for increased funds or resistance to discontinuing existing programs.

The restructure publicized the idea that a new kind of national church agency was being created. The constituency was told that for this new day, the church needed a new type of agency. The adoption of the plans of reorganization promised a different kind of bureaucracy which would be "better" than the old.

Efficiency and economy were themes constantly stressed by those wanting to restructure the bureaucracy. Thus expectations were raised, in some instances well beyond the level of reality. The "new" structure was in fact created out of the old. An organization that is created by the merger of three existing agencies brings together three distinct traditions and three professional staffs. The new title and mandate do not necessarily make a new organization. Furthermore, simply getting the new agency operating takes a larger portion of staff time during the first few years, leaving less time available for the primary work of the organization.

The anticipated better performance for less money has not been self-evident. When some agencies reported deficits in excess of a million dollars, the sense of disillusionment deepened. More funds are needed, so the pressure to increase contributions continues and with it the level of tension between the bureaucracy and its constituents.

The changes in the ways the national church agencies spend the money entrusted to them is the source of considerable controversy. To this topic we now turn.

Chapter 6
Fiscal Fiascoes

The way a national church agency spends its money is an important indicator of its values. The budget is where the theology of the organization is translated into specific programs and activities. The expenditures indicate the real priorities. Hence conflicts over the values and goals of an agency will occur over how the funds are allocated because it is the budget that makes the values concrete.

The finances of a national church agency are complex and often not understood by most members of their constituency. Even if an agency desires to be completely open regarding its finances, it has a difficult time communicating the data clearly to its clientele. If an agency wishes to be somewhat less than candid about its financial picture, the complexity of the situation makes this easy.

During the 1960s a shift occurred in the church bureaucracy's funding procedures. The movement was away from providing grants and services to local churches and institutions, which themselves were carrying on traditional ministries to people. Instead an increasing proportion of the agencies' monies was used to attempt to bring about changes in the society. The assumption was made that if changes could be made in the social and economic systems that were influencing the lives of people, particularly the disadvantaged, some of the problems which the individuals faced would be eliminated or at least reduced.

This chapter will focus on the agencies' finances, how the attitude toward the use of funds changed during the 1960s, and how the finances influenced and were influenced by the restructure of the church bureaucracy.

Supporting the Bureaucracy

There are two ways by which the national agencies attempt to insure continued financial support. First, each congregation is assessed or taxed a specific amount of money by the denomination. The size of this assessment is generally based on some formula that includes the number of members and the amount of money the congregation spends for certain items including the pastor's salary. By some method a figure of what a congregation of a particular size and strength should be expected to contribute to the national program is determined. Second, congregations are urged to contribute to specific projects and causes such as emergency relief, scholarships, colleges, settlement houses, new churches, individual missionaries, hunger, and other areas for which the agencies have responsibility.

While the assessment on the local church is voluntary, considerable pressure is exerted to see that the congregation meets its "fair share." There is strong peer pressure on the pastor to raise funds for denominational causes. Failure to support the general church programs is looked upon as a sign of disloyalty. The minister who for whatever reason fails to persuade his congregation to contribute to the denominational program is considered less than adequate both by his peers and his superiors. Pressure is also brought by denominational officials on the pastor. While pressure cannot effectively be brought upon the lay people, the minister is vulnerable. His career may be adversely affected if he fails to support the denominational program. He is particularly vulnerable in a church such as the United Methodist where he is appointed by the bishop. The pastor's success in getting his people to support the denominational program is an important factor in considerations involving promotion.

The first article of faith held by most bureaucrats is that church members can and should increase their contributions. They feel that if people were more committed to Christianity and more enlightened about what the agencies were doing, the amount of dollars would certainly rise.

The bureaucrat is caught in something of a dilemma in regard to the way funds are best raised. He wants as much money as possible to be given without any conditions attached. This allows the agency to determine how the funds shall be spent. It gives the staff maximum flexibility. Thus undesignated funds are preferred, those which are raised by the tax on congregations. Unfortunately there is always some local resistance to giving money in this manner.

People prefer to contribute to specific causes that they understand and with which they can identify. They like to feel that their gifts are accomplishing something specific. Foreign missions agencies have long understood this and have had returned missionaries visit churches to raise funds. Letters from missionaries are duplicated and used to maintain a personal relationship with contributors. The dilemma for the bureaucrat is that while undesignated funds give him the greatest amount of flexibility, they are the hardest to raise. Such funds depend on the general loyalty of the church members to their denomination, the credibility of the bureaucracy, and the effectiveness of the pressure that can be exerted on the clergy and on the congregations. Contributions designated for certain programs are easier to raise, but they can only be used for the designated purpose. A popular and well-publicized cause may have a surplus of

93

funds while an equally deserving, but little known, one may have insufficient support.

The church bureaucracy has tried to have it both ways. While the tax on the congregation remains the basic source of funds, individuals and congregations may also contribute to specific causes. Some of these causes have certain Sundays assigned on which a special offering may be taken. Other causes are officially designated as approved to receive contributions at any time. Thus the lay person may make a contribution to provide scholarships for American Indian students or to buy equipment for a particular missionary in Peru or Hong Kong. This has the effect of using popular causes to raise funds which then releases other monies for use elsewhere.

While the national church agencies are ultimately dependent on the good will and support of the members of the denomination, they are at the same time protected from direct pressure by their constituency. The funds that the agencies receive from the general tax on congregations are allocated by the governing body or by an agency to which this function has been delegated. Thus lay people contribute to their denomination which in turn divides the funds among the various parts of the bureaucracy.

When an agency becomes ineffective, out of touch with its constituency, or simply irrelevant, financial support is usually the last thing it loses. Unless the agency does something spectacular with which many church members violently disagree and that is widely reported in the news media, the financial support will continue, often for a number of years.

The national bureaucracy maintains one or more units whose task it is to see that the constituency is informed about the denominational program and therefore willing to continue to provide the necessary financial support. This is done with magazines, leaflets, brochures, filmstrips, records, and any other technique that might help get the message to the church members and ensure continued contributions.

The Bureaucrat and the Raising of Funds

Because the national church agencies are largely supported by voluntary contributions of lay people in the local congregations, it might be assumed that a bureaucratic leader would have the ability to raise funds or at least maintain good relationship with the givers. As the decade of the 1960s progressed, an increasing number of persons were brought into the agency staff who did not see raising money or even keeping on reasonably good terms with the rank and file clergy and lay people as their responsibility. These persons, many of whom were career bureaucrats, tended to look upon the average clergy and church members as adversaries rather than as a clientele to be served. The people providing the financial support for the agency activities ironically were perceived as representing the forces of reaction preventing the desired social changes. As the bureaucracy and their constituency pursued different goals, the level of conflict and alienation increased. Through all of this the assumption was made that these same church members would continue to provide the funds to support the bureaucracy.

The staff employed for public relations and fund raising continue to function as they always have, attempting to interpret the programs of the agencies in the best possible light so that the members will maintain their contributions. These promotional departments have tended to emphasize those activities which are most likely to be positively received by the constituents, hoping that the popular activities will offset those that the members find objectionable.

In the mid-sixties and continuing into the seventies, an increasing number of persons affiliated with the national church bureaucracy perceived the budget as a kind of personal or ideological allowance. They were trained to spend money; they did not see the necessity of maintaining the accountability with which the institution could assure continued support. The assumption was made that the institutional church would somehow always be there with the necessary funds.

This allowance mentality was particularly prevalent among certain special-interest groups. Endowed with an inferiority status that was translated into the right of special privilege (dignified by the word *compensatory*), such groups perceived the church as having an obligation to provide for their needs and support their interests. A reciprocal obligation of strengthening the institution was not part of the thinking of the special-interest groups.

In a prophetic article first published in 1968, Rodney Stark and Charles Y. Glock pointed out that church members with orthodox beliefs tended to be the financial supporters while those who accepted the social change theology of the Secular City were not significantly supporting the institution. They asked the question, "Will ethics be the death of Christianity?" Their answer is that the survival of the church is in great danger unless it can secure commitment from those who adhere to the new theology equal to those who hold orthodox views. The authors were not optimistic: "The new theologians have developed no consensus as to what they want the people to believe or to what kind of a church they want to build."[1]

In the final analysis a voluntary organization depends for

---

[1] Rodney Stark and Charles Y. Glock, "Will Ethics Be the Death of Christianity?" in *Religion in Radical Transition*, ed. Jeffery K. Hadden (New Brunswick, N.J.: Transaction Books, 1971), p. 84.

its continued existence on the loyalty and support of its membership. Church people tend to have a strong commitment to their church and considerable faith in its leaders. But as some parts of the national bureaucracy are discovering, their continued existence depends on the trust and support of the rank and file, a commodity that is not unlimited.

In the 1960s the national church agencies tended to shift their emphasis from funding traditional types of ministries and services to activities that were designed to produce certain social changes. Money that had gone into service institutions such as community centers and grants for pastors' salaries in mission-type churches was moved into such things as community organization and other social-change action programs. This was not done without resistance since the supporters of traditional ministries had and still have their supporters. The struggle still continues. The goals of the programs of the agencies have tended to shift to such items as "empowerment for a pluralistic society, minority self-determination and conscientization, and cultural awareness and affirmation."[2]

A number of factors converged to produce this change in the use of funds. First and foremost was the general acceptance of the theology of social change described in chapter 2. The persons saw the opportunity to be in on the ground floor in the development of the Secular City, and they quickly took an option.

Second, the civil rights movement was in full force. Church leaders legitimized by their presence the demonstrations that were taking place from Cicero, Illinois, to Albany, Georgia. The support of church people was needed and sought. For church bureaucrats it was an exciting time. They felt that they were not only the wave of the future, they were

---

[2]*National Division Docket* (New York: Board of Global Ministries, The United Methodist Church, 1974), p. 9.

determining the course of the future. And the civil rights movement was producing needed changes in the legal patterns of segregation that had plagued the nation for over a century.

Another important factor in the sixties was the discovery of training as a way to prepare persons to bring about change. The bureaucracy financed and engaged in a variety of enterprises to train church people to bring in the desired future. Examples of organizations which did this training were the Urban Training Center in Chicago, the Ecumenical Institute with headquarters in Chicago and branches in several cities, and the largely Methodist-financed, but ecumenically managed, Metropolitan Urban Service Training (MUST) in New York City. There were others, often with names that formed titles such as ACTS and COMMIT. Those doing the training did not lack confidence that they were preparing a cadre to lead the church in the emerging society. Much of the finances for these enterprises came from church agencies, either as direct grants or by underwriting the tuition and costs of trainees.

The riots in the urban ghettoes, which increased in intensity as the decade progressed, moved the attention from training and the traditional civil rights activities to a rethinking of the problems of the black population. The focus shifted to poverty and economic issues. It should be noted that the political leaders had already discovered the poverty problem. The federal war on poverty program was in full swing when the church agencies decided to enlist. The urban violence, which was occurring every summer, provided a sense of urgency and the feeling that the church must act immediately in new and bold ways.

So in the late 1960s the bureaucracy rushed into a new battle. Their financial resources were mobilized to solve the social and economic problems of the black ghettoes. By this time white leadership or even presence was no longer needed as had been the case in the earlier civil rights movement. Nevertheless, money was still wanted and needed. Black leaders discovered that churches had been instruments of oppression and provided a range of organizations to which restitution could be made in terms of financial grants. Minority empowerment became a popular slogan. Examples of the ways the churches used their resources will be discussed.

A Denominational Loan Program

An attempt of a national church agency to use its funds to achieve certain social and economic ends was the Mission Enterprise Loan and Investment Fund of The United Methodist Church. This organization became known as MELIC after the title of the board of directors, Mission Enterprise Loan and Investment Committee.

In January, 1968, the Board of Missions of The Methodist Church established a loan fund of not less than three million dollars for investment in ghetto areas and enterprises. The original motion described this action as "an expression of our concern particularly in the areas of racial and economic injustices. . . . Loans and/or grants are for enterprises planned, developed and managed by people entrapped in ghetto circumstances. . . . It is hoped that . . . such loans will provide for widespread ownership such as cooperatives and at the same time permit disadvantaged people to have a maximum feasible voice in their own economic enterprises."[3] Loans were to be made at the current prime rate of interest. The maximum loan could not exceed three hundred thousand dollars (10 percent of the fund). Criteria listed for qualifying

---

[3]"A Statement Regarding Mission Enterprise Loan and Investment Fund United Methodist Church," duplicated paper (June 11, 1968).

for a loan included such items as a sound plan, a strong desire to succeed as an independent businessman, evidence of sustained effort toward an objective, a willingness to work, and successful management experience.

Two types of loans were made by MELIC. The first was direct loans to applicants, mainly to start small business establishments in the black ghetto. The second type of commitment was one in which MELIC served as a third-party guarantor to selected banks in their relationship to the Small Business Administration. MELIC guaranteed a portion of certain loans, thus making it possible for the individual to borrow funds from a bank.

The loan applications were processed by the Methodist Board of Missions' National Division. No additional employees were added; the extra work was assigned to persons already on the staff. No provision was made for collecting the loans other than mailing a statement indicating the payment due.

By October, 1969, MELIC had committed or guaranteed loans totaling $1,654,040. Of this amount $787,140 were in direct loans and $866,900 were guarantees for loans from other lending institutions.

By 1970 problems were beginning to develop in collecting some of the payments. The Church Extension staff of the National Division whose major responsibility was the loans to United Methodist congregations was also given the task of collecting delinquent MELIC loans.

By the end of 1971, five companies which had borrowed money from MELIC had gone bankrupt with losses totaling $87,660. Five other loans totaling $347,145 were classified as having "very serious problems."

A year later, at the end of 1972, the number of bankruptcies had increased to seven and MELIC had lost $304,304. Losses ranged from $3,900 loaned to All American Chicken to $100,000 borrowed by The 10th Street Project.

100

Other organizations included a group in Michigan known as Young Men on the Move whose movement did not include repayment. Seven loans totaling $456,665 were classified as having "very serious problems."

As of December 31, 1972, there were twenty-one loans with a total principal amount of $1,194,500 and one guarantee of $7,500. Principal in arrears was $89,034. The loans had been made to persons in twelve states and the District of Columbia. Two loans were made outside the United States, one to a school in Indonesia, and another to a school in Zaire.[4]

In April, 1972, the Board of Missions discontinued the MELIC loan program. Attempts to collect the outstanding loans continued with varying degrees of success. One report stated: "One recurring problem that must be taken very seriously seems to be an inclination on the part of the recipients of these loans to see a debt to a church a little differently from a debt to a bank."[5]

The problems of collecting the MELIC loans continue. As of May 28, 1975, fourteen loans were delinquent. These outstanding loans totaled $695,244. The amount of principal past due was $126,772, and the amount of interest past due was $93,099.[6] Six loans totaling $433,226 were listed as having "very serious problems" in 1972. No payment has been received from any of these borrowers in the past two and one-half years.

The question that can be asked is what the MELIC program accomplished. On the negative side is the not inconsiderable outright loss of nearly three quarters of a million dollars. At the end of 1972, six months after the decision was made not to make any more loans, the amount of

---

[4]Mission Enterprise Loan Delinquency Committee, "Report for Year Ending December 31, 1973," duplicated paper (1973), pp. 1-3.

[5]*Ibid.*, p. 1.

[6]*National Division Loan Delinquency Report* (New York: Board of Global Ministries, The United Methodist Church, 1975).

money loaned to either companies which were already bankrupt or then in serious trouble totaled $760,969. It has been estimated that the losses ultimately will be somewhere between three quarters of a million and a million dollars.

On the positive side it can be said that a few businesses in the black ghetto received the funds which enabled them to get started. But this number is less than two dozen, hardly enough to make an impact on the hundreds of urban black ghettoes with their millions of residents.

Was the MELIC program a symbolic witness which demonstrated to the blacks that The United Methodist Church was concerned about their economic welfare? The answer has to be no. The program involved so few persons and organizations that only a very small number of blacks could have been aware of its existence.

Did MELIC demonstrate to white United Methodists that their church was concerned enough about economic opportunities for blacks to risk a sizable amount of funds? Here again the answer is no. This program was not given wide publicity, so it is probable that only a very small number of Methodist clergy and lay people were aware of its existence.

MELIC was not intended to be a symbolic program, but to make an impact on the black ghetto. It was instituted immediately after the 1967 riots in Newark and Detroit. There was a feeling that the church had to respond to the desperate situation in the nation. So the MELIC loan program was born, only to be a minor skirmish in the church's war on poverty from which the denomination soon withdrew, weaker, poorer, and probably none the wiser.

The major loss to the church is the annual income on the permanent funds loaned to businesses which have gone bankrupt. Thus the denomination's mission program will have approximately seventy thousand dollars less each year from now on, which represents the interest on the money lost.

102

Funding Self-Determination

The Episcopal Church responded to what was called "The Crisis in American Life" with a program that became known as the General Convention Special Program. This undertaking was to be highly controversial and a devisive force within the denomination. Opposition to it was so strong and widespread that it resulted in a sharp drop in income that necessitated a reduction in the national staff and programs.

Like similar undertakings in other denominations, this was in response to the urban riots. Prior to his departure for a meeting overseas, the presiding bishop instructed certain persons on his staff to prepare a program in response to the urban crisis. The staff decided to use the community organization approach by which the church would finance local groups.

The report to the General Convention described this:

> This program is not an "ecclesiastical war on poverty" . . . it is based on the principle of assisting the poor to organize themselves so that they may stand on their own feet, rise out of their degradation, and have full share in determining their own destiny. . . . The program affirms that they have the God-given capacity, if resources be supplied, to help solve the problems of which they have become victims in an affluent, industrialized, predominantly white society.[7]

The proposed program was discussed informally with a number of denominational leaders. It was then presented to the General Convention in Seattle as an amendment to the budget and adopted. A total of $2,265,917 was allocated for the urban crisis.[8]

A Screening and Review Committee was set up to process

[7]Journal of the General Convention (Protestant Episcopal Church, 1967), appendix 28.4.
[8]*Ibid.*, p. 230.

applications for grants. Seven members of this committee were "street people," persons from urban communities across the nation who might or might not have any connection with the Episcopal Church. Grants were made to a wide range of groups across the country, some of which were self-proclaimed revolutionaries and advocated violence to achieve their goals.

The crisis program, now known as the General Convention Special Program (GCSP), soon encountered opposition. The bishop of the diocese in which a grant was proposed was to be consulted in advance, but he had no veto. In many instances, he was not even informed. One staff person who was associated with this program commented, "The GCSP staff was too unwilling to compromise where it didn't matter. They were consistently antichurch and really set up an adversary situation with the local bishops."

As time passed, the opposition intensified. One large and influential congregation announced they would no longer support the denominational programs but give funds to projects which they would select. Another rector reported that the funding of a group in his city resulted in lay persons canceling twenty thousand dollars in pledges in a five-day period. He said, "In that week we lost the curate's salary and the new parish car." A diocese announced that the annual contribution to the denomination would be one dollar.

When the General Convention met in Houston, Texas, in 1970 it had received more than fifty memorials, resolutions, and petitions on the subject of the General Convention Special Program. Two actions were taken that limited the program. After affirming the original aims and purposes of the GCSP, the General Convention adopted the following:

> Provided that no grant under this program shall be made to any organization if such organization or any office or agent thereof advocates the use of physical violence as a means of carrying out the program of the organization. . . . The funding of any grant

shall be discontinued if the grantee shall be finally convicted of a crime which involves physical violence perpetuated in carrying out the program of the organization.[9]

The second action enabled the bishop to formally protest a grant in his diocese and have the grant reviewed by a higher body. The bishop was to be notified of the proposed grant and be sent a full copy of the grant application and full copy of the report of the staff appraisal. The bishop, with the consent of his executive board, standing committee, or dioesan convention, had thirty days to declare his opposition in writing. The denomination's Executive Council then ruled on the proposed grant, either upholding the bishop or the GCSP Screening and Review Committee.[10] In 1973 the GCSP was largely dismantled and the staff in charge left the employ of the church.

There is no consensus about the GCSP. Those who designed and supported it declare that it was the best church action program in the 1960s. They believe it demonstrated to the blacks that the church would stand with them and support them while helping to make the white church people sensitive to the needs of the black community. They cite the continuation of some of the activities started by the GCSP as proof of its value.

Those opposed to the program charge that grants were made to organizations that were ineffective and whose purpose and tactics were incompatible with the Christian faith. They contend that not only was much money wasted, but some actual harm was done. The drastic drop in denominational income and the reduction of the bureaucratic staff to the present corporal's guard is cited as a negative result.

---

[9]Journal of the General Convention (Protestant Episcopal Church, 1970), p. 301.
[10]*Ibid.*, p. 304.

During the period of the GCSP, approximately six million dollars in grants were made to a wide range of community organizations. It is impossible to demonstrate what effect those had on the urban crisis in America.

A Church-Sponsored Foundation

An ecumenical agency, the Interreligious Foundation for Community Organization (IFCO), was created in 1968 to provide a channel by which church and other money could be directed to black and other minority communities and self-help organizations. The director described it as "a church and community agency whose mission is to help forward the struggles of oppressed peoples for justice and self determination."[11]

Since its founding a variety of organizations have received grants through IFCO. Some examples from 1971 are: $10,564 for the American Indian Movement Center, Minneapolis, Minnesota; $24,326 for the Brotherhood Crusade, Inc., Los Angeles, California; a group described as a potential Black United Fund; $40,833 for the Delta Foundation, Inc. Greenville, Mississippi, a blue-jean factory using a former military barracks; and $329,800 for the Malcolm X Liberation University, Greensboro, North Carolina, a black technical institute that has since closed.

A large portion of the funds for IFCO comes from the national church agencies. Of a total income of $763,970 in 1971, church organizations contributed $517,197 or 67.7 percent. The three largest amounts came from The United Methodist Church ($178,822), the United Presbyterian Church in the U.S.A. ($153,000), and the United Church of Christ ($73,500).[12]

---

[11]*A Report of IFCO Concerns* (1973), p. 7.
[12]*IFCO Concerns* (1972), p. 14.

The income for 1974 was down to $599,805, but church agencies provided $359,907 or 60 percent. The largest amount came from the United Presbyterian Church in the U.S.A. ($173,000).[13]

The national church agencies have a large number of staff who are members of the IFCO Board of Directors. Eighteen of the thirty eight directors are employed by the church bureaucracy.

Beginning in 1971, IFCO made two important decisions. The first was to expand its activities outside the United States. The overseas program that has received the most funds is Relief for Africans In Need in the Sahel (RAINS). The second decision was to expand the technical assistance provided by the staff. In 1974, IFCO had an income of $599,805 but made grants of only $260,268, an amount equal to only 43.3 percent of the funds received.[14] The professional and nonprofessional staff now total sixteen. Several regional offices have been established. It would appear that IFCO is moving from a funding agency to a program agency that carries on activities itself.

IFCO tends to see its role as creating alternative institutions for America's minorities. In its annual report for 1972 the assumptions for such organizations are stated.

Government as we have known it is being systematically dismantled. . . . We know more than ever that white America as a whole never did take integration seriously. . . . Black capitalism was a joke from the start. . . . The long struggle for justice and liberation requires a stable, independent, alternative institution. Therefore in the 70's building independent alternative institutions will be a major activity of empowerment and liberation efforts in the United States.[15]

---

[13]*IFCO Annual Report (1975)*, p. 5
[14]*Ibid.*, p. 6.
[15]*IFCO Concerns* (1973), p. 9.

IFCO continues to be a kind of front by which large amounts of church funds are channeled by the national church bureaucracy to essentially secular agencies, chiefly community organizations and economic enterprises. Probably more than any other agency, IFCO epitomizes the ideology of social change devoid from any of the sources of Christian tradition. One cannot but wonder at the rationale by which funds raised for the Christian mission enterprise are used for grants to such organizations as the African Liberation Day Film, The Angola Film Project, The Committee for a Unified Newark, the Mississippi Association of Minority Attorneys, and the National Black Theater. While such enterprises may be socially useful and desirable, do they represent the best expression of the Christian mission?

Questionable Accomplishments

The increasing use of denominational funds to finance nonchurch organizations whose purposes are defined in economic and/or social terms is a logical application of the theological assumptions that were increasingly accepted by the leaders of the national church agencies in the sixties. If one accepts the idea that the goal of the church is to be an agency to assist in attaining social change and economic development, the kinds of programs that have been described in this chapter are acceptable strategies. If other assumptions about the church are held, these activities would be inappropriate for a denominational agency.

The great majority of lay people and large numbers of clergy who support the denominational agencies probably still think they are contributing to traditional ministries and services. The agencies have not been overly zealous to emphasize the change in direction, but have allowed the promotional departments to concentrate on programs that would be readily acceptable to the constituents. Nevertheless, tension over the difference in values and ideology appears to be increasing. The conflict that has erupted between the United Methodist Board of Global Ministries and the evangelical wing of the denomination is over the theology of the church and the purpose of the missionary enterprise. Other theological controversies are and will be occurring as more persons question the expenditures of the bureaucracy and begin to ask about the values that such expenditures represent. The debate over whether certain programs are appropriate for a church agency will continue.

In addition, the question can be raised whether these programs are effective in attaining their stated aims. At this time, the conclusion must be that the results of many of the church agency ventures into social and economic programs have not been particularly impressive.

It is important to note what the church agencies did not attempt to do by their venture into social and economic programs. They did not attempt to make a symbolic witness, to say to the larger society that it should consider similar activities because the church was by this action putting its stamp of approval on this type of undertaking. The people who led the agencies into these programs thought they had the capability of making a significant impact.

The church agencies were not engaged in experimental programs designed to develop models that would prove useful guides for other groups in the society. There were for the most part no evaluation procedures that would tell the agencies what was learned by the programs' successes and failures. One of the losses is that so little was learned. Thus it may not be possible to repeat the successes and avoid the failures.

Furthermore, many of the church's social and economic programs were started after the federal government had already launched its massive war on poverty. The timing of the church's efforts displays an attempt to jump on the

109

federal bandwagon. What is more significant than the fact that the denominational agencies were largely followers of government programs, is that their resources were such that they could hardly make a ripple in the sea of social and economic problems. Remember, the agencies were not engaging in symbolic action, not using their limited resources to call the attention of society to the problems. It was thought that a million and one-half dollars in loans to small ghetto businesses would make an economic difference and that a million dollars a year spread across several dozen groups in the United States (as in the case of the GCSP) or the world (as in the case of IFCO) would result in the kind of social changes that are still needed. That the results did not equal the expectations is not surprising and probably accounts for some of the current disillusionment.

Finally the programs described in this chapter were ones in which the church agencies operated from their weakness rather than their strength. They assumed a level of economic power that they did not possess. They tended to ignore the power that is inherent in the church, the prophetic witness, the concern with ultimate meaning and values, and the power of God in the lives of individuals and in the society.

The Christian church needs to confront injustices. It must attempt to bear a faithful witness among the complex systems which are oppressing people. But the way the church makes an impact on the larger society varies. The greatest influence of the church may not be when it acts as an institution but as it affects the values and actions of the millions of members. There are times when the church as an institution must bear witness and take specific actions. It must at the same time realize that its institutional resources are limited. The strength of the church is not in financial power; its strength is in faith that has sustained it in all types of social environments and economic systems and has enabled it to influence the lives of people and the course of society.

110

PART 3
ChANGiNG ThE BUREAUCRACY

Chapter 7
How Restructure Was Accomplished

The movement to restructure the national church agencies did not suddenly appear on the horizon in the late 1960s. There were early signs that changes in the church organization were coming. Some denominational leaders were expressing discontent with the church bureaucracy. They seemed convinced that the remedy was to reorganize the boards and agencies. Included among these were some board members and even a few staff executives.

Early in 1963 the Methodist Board of Missions appointed a committee to restructure that agency. Fourteen months later the proposed organization was passed by the denomination's General Conference, completing the first major changes in that agency in a quarter of a century. In the same year the United Presbyterian Church created a Special Committee on Regional Synods and Church Administration. This group functioned for six years and was followed in 1971 by the appointment of a Special Committee on General Assembly Agencies. Other denominations appointed groups to consider ways to change the national agencies. In 1968 the United Methodist General Conference selected a Structure Study Commission and the American Baptist Convention created the Study Commission on Denominational Structure. By the

111

end of the decade several other denominations had appointed special committees or commissions to design a new structure for their national agencies. These small groups were to make major changes in their respective denominational bureaucracies.

How these changes were accomplished will be the subject of this chapter. It will discuss the mandate given the special committees and commissions, how the groups functioned, what sources of information helped formulate their plans, what the areas of conflict and opposition were, and what compromises were necessary to assure acceptance of the proposals.

The Mandate

The mandates given the special committees varied, ranging from authorization to alter the basic organization of the denomination to only restructuring the national boards and agencies. The American Baptist Convention gave its Study Commission on Denominational Structure a broad mandate. The result was a range of changes that included the manner of electing delegates to the national body, the reorganizing of the national bureaucracy, and a new name. These changes may prove some of the most significant for that denomination in over half a century as it moves from a convention of congregations to a church.

The United Presbyterian Church in the U.S.A. and the Presbyterian Church in the U.S. restructured not only the national bureaucracy, but changed the size and number of synods, creating large regional synods. Thus the changes in the Baptist and Presbyterian denominations were closer to home for the average pastor and lay person than those in the other churches.

112

The Episcopal Church authorized a commission to consider a range of possible changes in the operation and structure of the denomination. In the final analysis financial pressure exerted a determining influence on what action was taken in regard to the national agencies. With a drastic and sudden decline in income, the national bureaucracy had to retrench. This process was accomplished in two stages; in each stage the number of employees was reduced because of a drop in support. The situation was not one in which a committee could with some degree of leisure consider the kind of national agencies that it wanted. It was an emergency requiring the dismissal of a large portion of the employees in order to be able to cover the payroll. These changes in the bureaucracy did not affect the organization of the diocese and had minimal effect on the average clergy or lay person, except that fewer services were available from the national offices.

The mandate given to the Structure Study Commission of The United Methodist Church was limited to reorganizing the national boards and agencies. It could not change the structure of either the regional annual conferences or the local churches. Thus its work did not have an immediate effect on the average minister or lay member.

Whatever else the special committees or commissions were authorized to do, they shared one common goal. Each had the clear mandate to recommend specific changes in the national church boards and agencies. The majority of the members not only were in agreement on this understanding of their task, they seemed to have a strong sense of responsibility to see that a new structure would be brought into being. Although the special committees were perceived by some to be "study" groups (two had the word *study* in the title), they were in fact action groups whose purpose was bringing about changes in their denominational bureaucracy.

113

The Responsible Group

The special committee or commission that was given the task of designing a new structure for the boards and agencies had certain common characteristics. The groups were small. The Ad Interim Committee of the Presbyterian Church in the U.S. began with twelve people to which a black and a Hispanic American were added a year later. The Episcopal Joint Commission on the Structure of the Church also had only twelve members. The American Baptist Convention created a twenty-three-member Study Commission on Denominational Structure, while the United Methodist structure commission began with twenty-two members to which four youths were added. The Commission on the Reorganization of the General Assembly Agencies of the United Presbyterian Church in the U.S.A. had thirteen members.

The small numbers placed a heavy responsibility on a few individuals. To deal with a range of issues, some divided into subcommittees. In the final analysis major changes in the church's structure were worked out by a half dozen or fewer persons.

The members tended to be broadly representative, if not of the rank and file, at least of the persons who make up the church legislative bodies and the board members. Each group included clergy and lay people. In the churches with an episcopal government some bishops were included. Prominent in the committees were persons who were or had been executives of the regional judicatories such as Methodist district superintendents or Presbyterian synod executives. Lay persons included a range of business and professional persons. An effort was made to have persons representative of ethnic and cultural minorities.

The members brought extensive experience in the church political process to their task, including experience with the bureaucratic structure. Many were persons who were used to

114

getting things done, both in the church and in the secular world. They were not only successful in designing a different structure for the national church bureaucracy, they were most effective in persuading the legislative bodies to adopt their proposals. Given the kind of persons to whom this assignment was given, it was evident from the beginning that something was going to be accomplished.

Influence of Key Persons

Within each group certain key persons exerted a strong influence on the style of operation and the proposals that were produced. The chairperson tended to have an important role in determining how such a committee functioned. Informal alliances within the group formed around issues. Differences among members were a source of tension and conflict. How opposing viewpoints were resolved often depended on the skill and fairness of the chairperson.

There is evidence that in every restructure committee a small group of elite leaders exerted a determining influence on the development of a new organization. An example occurred in the Structure Study Commission of The United Methodist Church. This group had strong opinions concerning what the new structure of the agencies should be. They had to struggle at times to keep the others in line. One person complained that at a meeting of the commission, the leaders had a difficult time convincing the other members to support a proposal. In the interval between meetings when these members would be subject to the influences of the clergy and lay people in their home areas, they would change their minds. At the next meeting, time would be lost counteracting the local influences and again persuading them to accept the plan of the leadership elite.

The close association of the members of the special

115

committees over a long meeting was frequent. One group met seven times in six months and another fifty-two times in a forty-four month period, which enabled them to know one another well. The members of one group suspected that a colleague had ambitions to become a staff executive in the proposed structure. To forestall this possibility, they took formal action that no member would be eligible for a position in the new organization for two years after its enactment.

A factor that is difficult to measure is the amount of influence that staff members employed by a special committee may have had. The members themselves were busy persons; all had other responsibilities. The task of designing of a new structure was time-consuming and much of the work had to be delegated to someone who could give adequate time to the job. The use of staff by the various groups varied.

The United Methodist Structure Study Commission employed a missionary on furlough as a full-time staff person. His absence from the United States gave him an aura of objectivity, although critics pointed out that as a missionary, he was employed by an agency subject to restructure. His office was only a few blocks from the church of which the chairman was pastor. This staff person appears to have had considerable influence, including the writing of the first draft of the legislation for the new structure.

Other denominations had somewhat different arrangements. Some were able to use the services of persons already employed by the denomination. While it is difficult to determine the extent of the influence of the staff member(s), such persons may have had a key role in determining the direction of the work of the commission. They did much of the day-to-day work. They prepared the position papers to which the members of the committee reacted. The members of the committee may have been able to decide in general what they wanted to accomplish, but it was the staff member who did much of the detailed work.

116

The Use of Consultants

At various points in the restructure process, the committees used the services of consultants, some from church-related organizations and others from commercial firms. While the employment of consultants varied, no group made extensive use of such services. There is no evidence that consultants had a determining influence on the design of the new structures.

The Episcopal Church engaged a well-known management consultant firm to study their organizations and make recommendations. When forced to reduce the number of staff members, this denomination employed another professional management consultant. The United Presbyterian committee engaged a firm to advise them on certain aspects of the proposed reorganization.

The United Methodist restructure of the bureaucracy was strictly a do-it-yourself undertaking. At only two points did this denomination's Structure Study Commission bring in outside persons. One of these was a professor from a theological seminary who prepared a short paper. Another was a university professor whose specialty was group process. He quickly uncovered some of the conflicts within the commission itself. Unwilling to allow the conflicts to surface, the group dismissed the consultant.

Consultants are utilized for several reasons. Such individuals might have information or skills in group process that help the committee achieve its goals. Outside persons may facilitate the group's task and enable it to achieve its goals with maximum efficiency in the minimum time. These are obvious reasons for engaging consultant services.

There are other less evident reasons. One is to provide a respite in the group dynamics. A committee may have a professor meet with them to read a paper on some aspect of their task. This provides a period of relaxation for the

117

members while giving the appearance of attending to the business at hand. An important church committee would hardly take the afternoon off to go to the movies; having a person from the outside do something can accomplish the same purpose in a socially acceptable manner.

Another contribution of the outside consultant is to legitimize the action of the employing group. One way of dealing with critics is to be able to cite the testimony of appropriate experts. A committee's proposals are strengthened if the members can point out that they were designed with the help of recognized experts and are presented with the full endorsement of such persons. Only the most courageous individual is likely to oppose the expert from afar who is assumed to be both knowledgeable and impartial. The critic may be convinced that the proposals are stupid, but he has no way of countering the appeal to expert judgment. He lacks information and the credibility to win acceptance of his differing viewpoint.

There are two possible reasons why the restructure committees did not make greater use of outside consultants. First, management consultants may have limited experience with church organizations. Some church leaders felt such services would not be worth the cost. A Presbyterian official commented that the assistance received from outside consultants was not worth the time required to brief them on the nature of the church and how it worked. He felt that the process was more an educational program for the consultant rather than a help to the church.

A second reason for not using more consultant services was that members of the restructure committees were experienced and knowledgeable church leaders who brought to their assignment definite ideas about the changes they wanted. Their goal was not to engage in a depth study but to get some specific things accomplished. Members may have felt that the services of an outside consultant were not

118

necessary. Furthermore, the input of such a person might actually have been dysfunctional because the issues that could be raised might delay the progress of the committee or move the group in a direction that would interfere with the attainment of the desired objectives.

Sources of Information

The members of the restructure committees would probably contend that they were correctly interpreting the will and the desires of their constituency. There is no question that the sentiment among a majority of the denomination's leadership favored making major changes in the church bureaucracy. The approval of the radical changes by the legislative bodies seems to verify that the special committees were correctly interpreting the sentiment of their constituencies.

The persons responsible for the restructuring used several methods to find out the opinions of the rank and file clergy and laity. One was through hearings in various parts of the country. The American Baptist Study Commission on Denominational Structure in a seventeen-month period held 135 "listening-interpretation" conferences with a total attendance of 6,325. This gave an average attendance of 48, a number small enough for questions, if not discussion.

The United Methodist group conducted similar hearings across the country. Arrangements were made by local judicatory officials who also were responsible for deciding whom to invite. Attendance was generally less than fifty persons.

A special session of the United Methodist General Conference was held midway in the life of the group. This gave the Structure Study Commission an opportunity to send a questionnaire to each of the delegates, the same persons

119

who had authorized their work two years earlier. The results of this questionnaire were included in an interim report.

A major source of data for all the restructure committees was the agencies themselves. This was a sensitive area. The members of these committees looked upon some board and all staff members with suspicion and apprehension. These persons were perceived as having the greatest vested interest in the *status quo* and hence most likely to frustrate proposed changes. Nevertheless, the committee members had to have certain information about the boards for which the cooperation of directors and staff was necessary. The committee members maintained a continual liaison with the bureaucracy. Some visited the agency offices and held meetings with the executives. Staff members were asked to prepare position papers; others sent unsolicited communications to the committees. Many bureaucrats were reluctant to reveal their true feelings, to seem hostile lest they be branded as self-seeking and opposed to a plan which would benefit the church.

In summary, the groups responsible for restructure did not attempt a systematic study. They relied on a variety of data, the chief of which seemed to be their own experiences and knowledge of their church. Information was gathered at public hearings and data were provided by the agency staff (although the latter was always suspect).

Ecumenical Relationships

With several denominations involved in restructuring at approximately the same time, the question can be raised as to whether the leaders shared information and experiences with each other.

The members of the special committees were aware that

120

the other churches were restructuring. There was some sharing of documents. For example, the chairman of one committee wrote to his counterparts in the other denominations and received various materials from them. There is no evidence that these documents were ever used.

An exception was the Presbyterian denominations. Because of the similarity and possible merger of these churches, considerably more communication took place between the groups responsible for restructure.

Nevertheless, the members of each denominational committee gave evidence of having a general understanding of what their counterparts were doing. The persons involved probably learned this through informal channels and the press. Several common factors run through each plan. These include the assumption that the bureaucracy needed to be trimmed down. In every plan the degree of centralization was increased, including concentrating some agency offices in one or more locations. Another common objective was greater coordination of programs.

It would appear that the similarity in proposals was due more to denominations being influenced by the same factors in society than by communication with each other. All were responding to the social turmoil of the 1960s. All were influenced by the theological trends of the period. All had the same antibureaucratic sentiment among their constituencies.

Despite this lack of formal communication, the action of one church was often used by another to justify a particular proposed action and to persuade the legislative body to adopt it. Criticism could be blunted if it could be pointed out that another denomination had independently decided on a similar course. For example, an argument used by United Presbyterian leaders to support the decision to centralize their agency offices in the Interchurch Center in New York was that the United Methodist offices were going to remain there.

121

Relationship with Constituencies

The restructure committees had six different constituencies with whom they had to maintain relationships.

The first constituency was the rank and file clergy and lay people, the general public of the denominations. Members of this group did not have a strong interest in the restructure of the bureaucracy as its effect on them was seen as minimal. These persons were primarily interested in the local church or, in the case of the clergy, in the regional judicatory. Nevertheless, the restructure committees had to keep these people informed. This they did by occasional articles and regular releases to the church press.

A second and more important constitutency was the professional staff and directors of the boards and agencies. The staff members were correctly perceived as the group most likely to be opposed to radical changes. This should not be surprising. Some had given many years of their lives in the service of the church through the national boards and agencies. A radical change in the structure could have drastic effects on them.

The employees of the agencies were the persons most likely to be called upon to make the personal sacrifices required by the implementation of the new plans of organization. While the new structure provided opportunities for some people, it wrecked the careers of others. Much of the hostility and resentment felt by the staff members was not due to the fact that they were having to make sacrifices, but because they felt such sacrifices to be in vain. Some felt the restructure would do more harm than good, a feeling that made their personal inconveniences and sacrifices more difficult to accept.

The staff members also felt that their experience and knowledge of the bureaucracy were not being utilized. This

122

was, at least in part, correct. While the restructure committees secured data from the agencies, they kept some distance between themselves and the agency personnel. The committees feared the power and influence of the staff and were determined to keep them from sabotaging their work.

The members of the boards were in a position somewhat similar to the staff, the difference being a matter of degree. They also were perceived as having a vested interest in perpetuating the work of their agency. The relationship between the restructure committees and board members and staff was one of continual conflict which varied only in degree throughout the time when the new structure was being designed.

A third constituency was the key politically oriented clergy in the regional judicatories. These included annual conference and synod executives and pastors who occupy the offices in these organizations. Such persons were important for two reasons. First, they were the primary clients of the bureaucracy, those most likely to utilize the services of the national agencies. Thus they had a strong interest in the kind of organizations to be developed. Second, these persons are often included among the delegates to the national legislative assemblies. Their support was necessary to assure the final passage of the plan of reorganization.

Continued contact between the restructure committees and members of this group was essential. Much of it was on an informal basis as the persons on the committees reported to the people in their home areas. Many of the participants in the hearings that some denominations held across the country represented this group.

A fourth constituency was the ordained elite. Included in this group were the bishops in those denominations that have this office and certain highly influential clergy. Most of the latter were pastors of large and influential congregations

123

although some were found in other positions such as presidents of colleges or theological seminaries. A few were regional executives. All held important and highly influential posts in their denominations. All were highly respected in their regional judicatory and many had denomination-wide influence as well. The restructure committees had to be careful to maintain a close relationship with persons in this group. This was done on an informal basis.

A fifth constituency was the key lay people. Members of this group are not highly visible; in fact, they may be virtually anonymous as far as the average minister and church member are concerned. Such persons are found on the boards of trustees of the church colleges, retirement homes, and other institutions. They tend to be individuals of means and many have substantial wealth. They operate behind the scenes and are able to get things done. Their advice will be sought and likely followed by the denominational executives. The support or the lack of it by members of this group can mean the difference between the success or failure of a particular denominational undertaking. A number of lay members of the restructure committees were persons in this group, a fact which facilitated communication and helped win support for the passage of the plans of reorganization.

A sixth constituency with which the restructure committees had to be concerned was the special-interest caucuses. These are highly visible and sometimes noisy groups whom the committees saw as potential allies. In any case, they did not want any organized group openly demonstrating against them. The United Methodist Structure Study Committee made an early attempt to win the support of the caucus groups. The Youth Caucus was supportive from the beginning, apparently on the theory that anything that promised to shake up the "establishment" could not be all bad. The Women's Caucus also favored the reorganization because

124

quotas for women staff members were written into the proposed legislation.

The Political Process

The restructuring of the boards and agencies of a Protestant denomination was essentially a political process. A plan had to be devised that was acceptable to a wide range of people, some with divergent interests. An electorate in the form of a national legislative body had to be persuaded to approve the proposed plan. In the process there were conflicts and compromises, heroes and villians, winners and losers. The important decisions were not always in public view on the floor of the national assemblies but in the church's equivalent of the smoke-filled rooms.

The committees responsible for the restructure of the boards and agencies did not simply design a new organization, the members struggled with each other to produce a plan that would achieve their goals and still win the necessary approval. Any proposal would inevitably arouse some opposition. The first source of opposition was within the committees themselves. Not all members were in complete accord and some even fought against the proposals down to the last vote before the matter was put before the legislative assembly.

Opposition can be successfully handled in two ways. The recalcitrant members can simply be voted down, particularly if they are few in number and do not have sufficient power to prevent the desired goals. The opponents can be won over, or at least neutralized, by some type of compromise. The restructure committees used both techniques.

It is impossible to chart the kind of internal struggles that took place within the committees. From the correspondence between certain members and the chairman of the United

Methodist Structure Study Commission, it is possible to understand the extent of opposition and the issues around which it focused. While the group was able to produce an acceptable proposal some members maintained their minority position until the end.

Opposition from groups outside the restructure committee was a threat. They could have vetoed the proposed reorganization of the bureaucracy, making compromises a necessity.

The persons most opposed to the restructure were some executives and professional staff members of the boards and agencies. Some were unable to have any influence on the course of events; others secured advantages for their agencies. Many executives correctly felt that their knowledge and expertise were being ignored. A layman employed as a chief executive was convinced that serious mistakes were being made, but he was unable to get a hearing for his views.

Effective opposition was handled by compromising. In The United Methodist Church opposition surfaced in two powerful agencies, the Council on World Service, which allocates denominational funds, and the Board of Missions. This could have derailed the proposed restructure. The compromise was to change the names of these agencies to the Council on Finance and Administration and the Board of Global Ministries but otherwise leave them intact and even stronger. Two smaller agencies, the Board of Health and Welfare and the Commission on Ecumenical Affairs, became divisions of the Board of Global Ministries, making it the largest unit in the United Methodist bureaucracy. The other parts of this denomination's agencies were unable to organize effective opposition and as a result were completely reshuffled. The final result was a bureaucratic structure that was not the product of logic but the political art of the possible; rational goals were altered by the fires of compromise.

Adoption and Alteration

The final test of the acceptability of the proposed plans of restructure was the willingness of the denominations' legislative bodies to give approval. The proposals would result in major changes for the denominations. For The United Methodist Church it was to mean a scrambling of the national agencies. For the American Baptists it was to mean basic changes in the form of representation as well as a reorganization of the bureaucracy. For both Presbyterian denominations it was to mean a complete overhaul of the agencies and changes in the regional synods.

Some members of the restructure committees took an active part in the campaign to get their proposals adopted. In the several months prior to the meeting of the United Methodist General Conference, the Structure Study Commission mounted an effective campaign to get its plan approved. Someone from the commission arranged to visit each annual conference and to meet with those persons who were delegates to the national body. An attempt was made to send persons who would be compatible with the people with whom they were to meet, or as it was described by a participant, "home folks to visit with home folks." When the member of the commission met with the delegation, he was to observe who the leaders and opinion-makers were and determine where they stood on the issues. He was also to decide who should receive some follow-up cultivation such as a letter or a telephone call.

The effort to line up votes continued during the session of the General Conference. Members of the commission carefully watched the various committees of this body to determine who the members were and where lobbying was most needed. The success of their efforts is attested to by the fact that the proposed plan of reorganization was passed by

127

the General Conference with only minor changes. An article in the church press carried the title, "They Can't Believe They Passed the Whole Thing." While there was surprise at the ease with which the new structure was adopted, the battle had in fact been won before the delegates left home.

There is some question whether a complex proposal worked out by a special committee over a period of time, such as a plan for reorganization of the denomination's national bureaucracy, can be effectively altered by the legislative body. The national assembly has the power to do this; however, major changes are rarely made. The delegates meet for only a short time, generally less than two weeks. They have a large number of complicated matters with which to deal. They do not have time to redo a carefully prepared complex piece of legislation. Because those who served on the special committees are honorable and capable people, the delegates are likely to accept their recommendations. This does not mean that there will not be questions, amendments, and often heated debate. Some minor changes will almost certainly be made. Occasionally even a major change will inadvertently be proposed and passed. In the final analysis passage is virtually assured if the members of the special committee or commission have done their work well, have prepared a sufficiently comprehensive and complex report, assured the group that they have consulted knowledgeable church leaders and appropriate experts, and done adequate lobbying in advance.

The legislative body really has only two choices. It can approve the proposals with minor alterations, or it can reject the whole thing. The latter would seem to be an enormous waste of manpower and money and an affront to the people who worked long and hard to prepare the plan. Given the way church bodies operate, the probability of approval is high.

Review and Evaluation

The restructure committees were aware that the plans of reorganization that would be adopted by their respective national assemblies would do less than create the perfect bureaucratic structure. There seemed to be an uneasy feeling that the evils that had been present in the old bureaucracy might reappear in the new. Duplication of programs, lack of coordination, inefficiency, and even "bureaucratic kingdom building" might somehow appear in the future. Thus the restructure committees attempted to build into the new organization some method of review and evaluation.

Church organizations have a particularly difficult time with review and evaluation. This requires hard decisions, sometimes making negative judgements about individuals. Church people by nature want to be helpful, to bring out the best in individuals. They find the evaluation process distasteful.

Furthermore, the matter of review tends to have another problem when it is applied to the church boards and agencies. These organizations are governed by a board of directors who are responsible to the people who elected them. The directors hire the professional staff and determine the policies of each of the agencies. If they do not like what the staff of the agency is doing, they have the authority to demand that the situation be changed. Therefore an agency to review and evaluate the bureaucracy means another group, selected by the same or a similar process and representing the same constituency, has the job of looking over the shoulders of the members of the other boards and their professional staffs. This means the creation of more bureaucracy. Furthermore, there is no assurance that the judgment of the persons selected to conduct the review and evaluation will be appreciably better than that of the individuals whom they are evaluating.

Two types of evaluation procedures are in use. The first is

illustrated by the Evaluation Team of the Presbyterian Church in the U.S. A three-person team has been employed to look over the shoulder of the staff of the General Executive Board of that denomination. This group reviews and evaluates the work of the program divisions and reports directly to the General Executive Board, which then can take whatever action it deems appropriate. In this case one small group of professional staff members monitors the performance of a larger number of others. Both groups are responsible to the same board of directors.

The second type of evaluation and review procedure is for these functions to be assigned to an independent agency that has both a board of directors and a professional staff. This is the system used in The United Methodist Church where the review and evaluation of the boards and agencies have been delegated to the General Council of Ministries. This body is made up of 125 persons who are broadly representative of the constituency of the denomination. Six persons constitute the professional staff. This represents the creation of an agency that is supposed to watch the other parts of the bureaucracy. In its first three years it did not challenge a board or agency on any significant issue.

The Protestant denominations spent thousands of man-hours and millions of dollars reorganizing their national agencies. What happened as a result of this considerable effort is the subject to which we now turn.

Chapter 8
What the Church Is Doing in Bureaucracy

During a ten-year period the denominations spent vast sums of money reorganizing their national agencies. In less than four years the United Methodist Structure Study Commission spent $231,211.36, largely travel and meeting costs. If the indirect costs in staff time and energy diverted from other activities could be calculated the amount would be much larger. What was accomplished by this use of a large amount of time and money? Were the perceived problems solved and the desired goals attained?

This chapter will examine a number of factors now present in the church related to the restructure of the bureaucracy. Some are the direct result of the reorganization; others existed prior to restructure, and both influenced and were influenced by that process. Each will be treated from three perspectives: (1) the perceived problems that the restructure was supposed to alleviate, (2) the desired goal that would solve the problems, and (3) the consequences of the actions that the denominations took.

Efficiency and Economy

Efficiency and economy are acceptable and usually explicit objectives for reorganizing a church agency. It is generally assumed to be possible to find a better way to do almost anything. Those paying the bills are always eager to hear that a performance equal to or better than the present one can be achieved for less money.

The committees responsible for restructure acted on the assumption that the church bureaucracy had certain inefficiencies that could be eliminated, thus improving performance and cutting costs. The committees did not do studies in depth that could pinpoint the presumed inefficiencies and find ways to correct them. There was, however, the assumption that new sophisticated management methods and equipment could accomplish greater efficiency and economy. Restructure was to facilitate their use.

It is not evident that the shifts in structure have made or will make a significant difference in either economy or efficiency. Actually the church bureaucracy had been making use of computers and other new management techniques prior to restructure. One consequence of this, unrelated to the reorganization, has been the increased need for technicians who are experts in operating the equipment. The staff members whose experience and orientation is toward people and programs may become a prisoner of the sophisticated hardware. An example was the interchange between a constituent and a bureaucrat. The constituent wanted to know the amount of funds the agency had contributed to a controversial program. The staff member said the data were in the computer and unavailable. The person making the request was incensed, feeling he was getting the runaround; for the bureaucrat, the response was logical. The data were in the computer, and he could only secure them by having the appropriate technician put aside other work and extract it from the machine's memory banks. The answer which seemed so logical to the bureaucrat did not make sense to the constituent who thought the church agency should be able to tell him how the money was being spent.

No definitive answer can be given to the question of whether the restructure of the bureaucracy will ultimately save money. Because it is impossible to accurately measure the output of a church agency, it is impossible to determine whether one kind of organization is doing an equivalent amount of work for less money than is one using a different style. However, the claims of economy, where they are made in connection with the reorganization of the church bureaucracy, are a myth. The restructure meant the relocation of literally hundreds of employees. This is an expensive process in terms of office remodeling, moving costs, training replacements for the clerical and other employees who did not move, and termination benefits for those who resigned or were discharged. If it could be calculated, the actual dollar costs of the restructure would be enormous. Whatever economies might have been achieved will have to be practiced for decades to offset the real cost of the reorganization.

There is a need for better financial management in the church agencies. This is not related primarily to the cost of operating the headquarters' offices but to the need to develop a way of cost accounting the programs of the agencies and the causes they subsidize. Some methods, imperfect though they may be, of relating what is expended to the achievement of the desired goals are needed. An obvious area where this is necessary is when several units of a denominational bureaucracy contribute funds to the same program, a common practice in The United Methodist Church. A result may be a large amount of funds from the same denomination going into a particular cause or organization with little opportunity to relate the amount of subsidy to the results.

Style of Operation

The problem to be solved by restructure was the perceived authoritarian style of the agencies. The objective was to

133

create a more collegial style of both board and staff operations, one in which there would be the maximum participation of all persons involved. A result is more time spent in board and staff meetings. An example is the National Division of The United Methodist Board of Global Ministries where the entire professional staff meets for an entire five-day week each month during nine months of the year. Some thirty-five persons spend a minimum of forty-five days, one-fourth of their working time, talking to each other. An agency turns inward as more energy is expended on the internal processes rather than on the services that might be provided to the churches. Another consequence has been indecisiveness. With an emphasis on a collegial process, needed decisions do not seem to get made in what could be considered a reasonable amount of time.

Related to the perceived authoritarian staff style was a general distrust of staff experts who, it was felt, had a tendency to create a kind of private fiefdom within the bureaucracy. The restructure of the church agencies has had the effect of downgrading the value of expertise. It has done this by shifting the structure in such a way that some specialized departments have been replaced by task forces. Staff members are expected to be flexible, giving their time to a task force working on whatever issue happens to be on the agenda of the denomination or the agency at a particular time. They are not experts, but enablers.

This approach was used by the Episcopal Church in the reorganization of the Executive Council Staff in 1970. The criteria for staff selection included: "Persons who understand that the core of the job involves the entire team (no room for prima donnas for there will be limited areas for the exercise of specialties). . . Experienced "hands" accustomed to serving many bosses in a multitude of tasks."[1]

---

[1] "Reorganization of the Executive Council Staff," duplicated paper (Executive Council, The Episcopal Church, 1970), p. 3.

Individuals are expected to function in a wide range of areas, some clearly beyond the reasonable level of competency of any one person. The result has been frustration on the part of the staff who know their own limitations and unhappy constituents who expect a level of expertise that they are not receiving. The requests to the national agencies are and will continue to be specific and technical. The person coming to an agency wants help on a particular problem. When he cannot get it from what is assumed to be the appropriate source, he becomes angry and wonders why the church should continue to support an organization that is not doing its job.

The restructure committees also felt that too many decisions were being made by staff. The way to solve this was to design an organization in which more decisions would actually be made by the members of the boards of directors. This has been done. The board members are in fact involving themselves in all aspects of the work of the agency, but the results are not necessarily happy. The problem is that the directors are getting involved in the ordinary day-to-day operations that should be delegated to staff. A result is not only an inefficient use of staff but a cumbersome way of trying to run an organization. One official commented on why the directors tend to give their attention to trivial matters.

> We give these people [the board members] some awesome responsibilities. You hand a guy a report like we did last year asking about the church's use of the ordained ministry. Are we getting the right kind of people? . . . Are we helping them develop throughout their lifetime in the places they can serve best? . . . You hand them that report and they juggle it like a hot potato. They get into it a little and realize what they're talking about is the theological function of the priest of God. And they end dealing with a new set of forms on which to get information.

The restructure has had significant and varied effects on the operating style of the agencies. The desire for a participatory and collegial style has resulted in some agencies placing a disproportionate emphasis on the manner of doing the work rather than on what actually is accomplished. Certain larger organizations have become more authoritarian as decisions are made by a very small group. The style of the bureaucratic operations has been changed by the restructure; it has not necessarily been improved.

Distributing the Power

Whatever else the restructure of the church bureaucracy was about, one of its major objectives was to change the distribution of power. There were two parts to this goal. The first concerned the power to control the church boards and agencies themselves. The second dealt with the power that the bureaucracy itself exercised in the church. A change in the distribution of power was to varying degrees achieved by the reorganization.

The major change regarding the control of the agencies themselves was the attempt to include a minimum number of women and members of certain ethnic and cultural groups in both board and staff positions. Board members are still selected by the regional judicatories except they are now more broadly representative of the various groups within the general constituency. This has meant the exclusion of some persons who have traditionally given leadership to the church agencies. The positions on the boards of directors of the church agencies are still won by a political process except that certain persons have now been given an advantage.

The reason for wanting to control the bureaucracy is to have access to the power that the agencies are perceived to have by the church. The effect of the restructure on the power wielded by the agencies is both varied and complex. To understand the present situation, it is necessary to note that there was both a centralizing and decentralizing trend going on simultaneously. The agencies themselves were being centralized while units were merged into fewer and larger agencies. The emphasis was on control, coordination, and accountability. Some positions were given limited tenure. The denominations established agencies whose task was to watch the other parts of the bureaucracy and to intervene if a particular agency was exceeding its authority or duplicating the work of another.

At the same time that the bureaucratic structures were experiencing a greater degree of centralization, some denominations, particularly the Presbyterians and Baptists, were decentralizing their functions. Some of the functions previously assigned to the national bureaucracy were delegated to the regional judicatories which then decided what they wanted to do about continuing the programs or providing the services. This represented a decrease in the power of the national bureaucracy. The Episcopal Church discontinued a number of functions that the national bureaucracy had performed. The United Methodists simply merged various agencies, thus delegating the decisions concerning the discontinuance of programs and services to the successor agencies.

Centralizing several units into one tends to concentrate more power in that agency, although it may represent a decrease in total bureaucratic power. Centralization also tends to focus responsibility. Constituents know whom to blame if things go wrong. The recently created formal methods of monitoring the agencies represent a further decrease in the power of the church bureaucracy.

Power in the bureaucracy is related to money, which enables staff to be employed, programs to be funded, and subsidies to be provided. A point of continued struggle in the denominations is the allocation of the benevolence funds. The struggle exists at two levels. The first is among the various units of the bureaucracy over what proportion each agency will receive. The second is between the national agencies and the regional judicatories over what amount shall remain in the local areas and what shall be sent to the national agencies.

In a time of declining income, the struggle between the agencies over the allocation of church funds may become intense and bitter. An organization's share may mean the difference between its survival or death. With peoples' careers at stake and the future of the programs and institutions in jeopardy, every agency will attempt to secure adequate funding. Conflicts between agencies will be intense in a period of declining income.

The controversy over the share of the available funds to be retained by the regional judicatory and the proportion to be sent to the national agencies will continue but is generally less open than that between parts of the bureaucracy. Because the funds come from the local level, the national agencies cannot afford to alienate the local officials to a degree that they will not support their work. The regional church leaders on the other hand are generally unwilling to appear uncooperative in their support of their denominational program.

For several years the denominational leaders have been urging the local churches and regional judicatories to be "in mission" in their communities. The restructure shifted some of the services from the national agencies to the regional organizations. Both local mission projects and services require money. As the competition for available benevolence funds increases, the temptation and the pressure to keep more of the money at home will increase. There will be less willingness to send funds to the national office if the bureaucracy is not providing services for the churches and support for local projects, especially when it can be legitimately argued that the funds are needed for worthwhile local projects. The competition between the national bureaucracy and the regional judicatories for the benevolence money will be an issue facing church leaders for the indefinite future.

Overall, the restructure seems to have resulted in a concentration of authority in the bureaucracy but in an overall decrease in the power of the national agencies. The loss of functions and programs to the regional judicatories, the formal review and evaluation of performance, the restrictions placed on staff, and the probable loss of funds to regional judicatories are evidences of the loss of power.

A Naked Political Process

Decisions in the church are made by a political process. A representative body is elected by the constituency. Leaders are selected and given the authority to act in prescribed areas. Struggles for leadership positions take place between rival groups and individuals. The contenders must know the rules of the game and play by them.

Within the church the political process has traditionally been very low key, if not hidden from the general view. Church leaders and certain insiders knew the system and how to work it, but the average church member did not understand or care how their denomination operated. In some denominations the individual did not openly seek high office but waited, as it was sometimes put, "for the call of the church." This did not preclude someone from having his friends work to secure the desired position for him. To be obviously seeking office, however, meant almost certain failure. Such explicit ambition seemed inconsistent with a call from the Lord.

The restructure of the national agencies is part of a change in the political process of the religious bodies. Events of

139

recent years have tended to politicize the church so that struggles for power are more visible. The attempt to gain control is less likely to be hidden behind the facade of unanimity. The national church bureaucracy has been the scene of battles for control of the denominational resources. The rules are changing, and it is not yet certain what they shall be.

A problem to which the restructure committees addressed themselves was the control of the agencies. The underlying assumption was that the church was controlled by forces that represented a leadership elite whose continuance in power was assured by the old political rules of the game. Those opposed had participatory democracy as a goal. This meant, in practical terms, having the maximum representation by the maximum number of different kinds of people. As a bureaucracy must be operated by a relatively small board, a symbolic participatory democracy in the form of broadening the base of representation, had to suffice. The quotas based on sex, age, race, and cultural groupings were visible signs that all of the important elements in the constituency were represented.

In considering this aspect of the restructuring, it is helpful to note that the term "empowerment" was frequently used. This meant that persons and groups previously without power were to be somehow endowed with it. While power may not be a finite commodity, it was necessary to reduce the power previously held by some groups to symbolize that different groups did in fact now have power. The restructure of the national agencies accomplished this. An example is the way the leadership role of United Methodist bishops in that denomination's bureaucracy has been dramatically reduced. The number of bishops on the boards has been curtailed. In the coordinating agency they may not hold office. One veteran staff member commented:

You used to have a bishop as chairman of your departmental committees. Now you may get a Chicano or a housewife who have had not any experience and don't have the foggiest idea of what they are to do.

It was inevitable that the focus of this political process would be in the struggles for control of the national bureaucracy. Here is the only arena in which the winners could gain control of some significant amount of tangible spoils in the form of high-status jobs and funds for programs and projects. The control of the means of communication lodged in the bureaucracy is perceived as a way by which the special interest groups can further their causes.

It is still not certain whether those who are attempting to politicize the church will ultimately prevail. The openly political style is repugnant to many clergy and lay persons on whose support the bureaucracy rests. Some feel that much of the time and energy going into the struggles for position and control of the denominational machinery is being spent on the wrong battle and not furthering the Christian cause. The declining income and continued distrust of the national agencies are a further indication that to be an effective leader in a Protestant denomination, more is required than simply winning a majority of the votes. The "more" in this case includes the personal charisma of the leader, the ability to win and maintain trust, and the skill to achieve prominence without violating the denomination's traditions in a manner that will alienate the constituency.

The Creation of the Superboard

One of the results of the restructuring of the national church bureaucracy was the consolidation of agencies into a fewer and larger organizations, thus creating the super-board. Such agencies are made up of five or more major

141

divisions which have a range of divergent responsibilities. The actual work of some of the subsections may have little relationship to each other except that they are governed by the same board of directors.

Several problems seemed to have resulted in the creation of the superboards. The first was the perceived wasteful and needless duplication of programs by different agencies within the same denomination. Consolidation seemed the obvious way to remedy the situation. The agencies that emerged generally had some logic although the final result was as likely to be influenced by established traditions, political compromises, and the protection of bureaucratic turf. For example, the United Methodist Board of Global Ministries has a unit whose responsibility includes church-related hospitals. Another division also has responsibility for several hospitals. The reason for this is not logic but tradition. The latter unit with responsibility for only a few hospitals was once an independent mission board and as such had established and partially supported hospitals for under-privileged people. The former was a separate agency with responsibility for church-related hospitals across the country. Despite the merger, two different parts of the same organization with offices actually on the same floor, continue to have a responsibility for church-related hospitals.

The creation of the superboards has changed the way such agencies function. Because the managers have a large number of units to supervise, there have been more frequent meetings. The General Executive Board of the Presbyterian Church in the U.S. meets five times a year. The United Methodist Board of Global Ministries meets twice a year; its predecessor met annually. This has greatly increased the cost, not only the actual expenses of the meeting but the amount of staff time needed for preparation. As one Presbyterian executive put it, "You seem to have just finished with one meeting of the General Executive Board when you discover it is time to start getting ready for the next."

Another consequence of the larger boards is the greater problem of communications between the various subunits. Because of the size of such an agency and diversity of functions, the staff of some of the different subsections may have virtually no communication with each other. The same is true of board members. The problem of internal communication in a large group is simply more difficult than in a small.

A second problem was the perceived lack of accountability of certain national boards and agencies. These organizations could act with a degree of independence that permitted them to duplicate the programs of other parts of the bureaucracy, engage in activities of which large parts of the constituency disapproved, or fail to initiate activities that were considered desirable. By combining agencies and making the various departments and their respective staffs responsible to one board of managers, the lines of accountability were to be clear and such abuses thus eliminated.

The decisions concerning programs are now concentrated in fewer groups. The directors of a superboard must govern a complex organization with many diverse parts. Because of the size of the superboards, the professional staff has less contact with the directors. An additional layer of bureaucracy has been created between the professional staff and the board members. Thus the directors deal primarily with the senior executives who interpret their decisions to the lower level staff. The executives become a kind of filter through whom the desires and needs of the constituency, as interpreted by the directors, are passed onto the staff. This has increased the power of the executives. It has also increased the alienation of the lower-echelon staff members as they have less opportunity to have direct contact with the directors of the agency for which they work.

Where accountability is lodged is more clearly defined in

the new structures than it was in the old. It also appears to be making the bureaucracy more authoritarian and impersonal. The executive may feel he has less room to maneuver and be inclined to make arbitrary decisions. The board members who deal primarily with the executive can make decisions without being directly involved with the staff person most affected. The arbitrary dismissal of staff members is made easier in the superboards because the larger organizations are more impersonal.

The superboards are still relatively new. Their establishment has resulted in some, but not all, of the desired changes in the church agencies. But they also have their negative side, *i.e.*, a more authoritarian management style, an increased alienation of staff from board members, and the creation of another layer of bureaucracy.

Collegiality and Quotas

A legacy of the reorganization of the church boards and agencies has been the formal and informal quotas for both board members and professional staff. The formal quotas provide that a certain proportion of persons be drawn from particular groups in the population such as women, blacks, and other ethnic and cultural minorities. Such requirements are now mandatory for certain agencies.

Informal quotas represent the pressure put on each agency to see that there is representation of the appropriate population groups on the board of directors and in the various levels of the executive and the professional staff. This representation is not necessarily in proportion to the number of persons of each group in the constituency of that denomination. Each agency must have a number of persons in important positions who are not white, ordained, English-speaking men. The pressure on the agency executives to see that their staff meets the formal and informal quotas is intense. The excuse that an appropriate person to fill a quota did not apply for a vacant position is not acceptable. The executive is to take "affirmative action," *i.e.*, find someone. The United Presbyterian Church has taken action that failure of an executive to find and employ minority persons shall be grounds for dismissal. A reason cited for locating the United Presbyterian agencies in New York was the concentration there of a range of ethnic and cultural groups from which persons could be employed.

A problem that the quotas were to solve was the lack of representation of all significant segments of the membership of the denominations. To correct this, formal quotas were established to give a voice to a wide range of people and strengthen the connection between the diverse elements in the constituency. The informal quotas seem to be a result of the guilt felt by liberal church persons over past injustices.

The denominational leaders did not trust the general constituency to elect what was considered an adequate number of women and minority persons to membership on the boards and agencies. A formal quota assured a minimum number, useful for consciousness raising during a period of transition. It was assumed that over the long run quotas would become unnecessary as the constituency became more sensitive to the need of having all the groups represented in the bureaucratic leadership.

Priority has been given to having the desired representation. Competence was to become—at least temporarily—a secondary requirement. Thus the goal has been to find a person who first could fill the desired quota, not the most competent one. Hopefully the individual of the desired sex and/or race would also have the skills to do the job. The first consideration has clearly not been skills but sex and/or race. One senior black staff member, in response to an inquiry concerning the lack of minority persons with certain needed

145

expertise, said: "Many of those jobs have been held by incompetent whites. There is no reason why they should not now be given to incompetent blacks."

Another perceived problem was the new tasks that the church was facing in the 1960s. It was correctly felt that certain positions could only be filled by someone who was a member of a particular ethnic minority. The growing racial pride and ethnic nationalism spelled the end of the old-style missionary executive. No longer could even a sensitive and well-meaning white preside over the Hispanic congregation or the Native American judicatory. It was also felt that those persons responsible for directing denominational strategy in the urban centers with their large black populations should themselves be members of that group. Thus one motivation for the selection of persons who are members of ethnic minorities was to increase the level of staff competence in dealing with new situations arising out of the changing social scene.

The formal and informal quota systems have changed the manner by which staff members relate to the agency in which they are employed and to each other. The person who gets a position because of his or her sex or race and with the assistance of a caucus will tend to have a primary loyalty to the group that he or she represents rather than to the agency or the general constituency of the denomination. It is natural for an individual to be loyal to the group responsible for his being employed in what is perceived to be a high-status job. Thus the purposes for which the agency was established may be subverted to the goals of a particular caucus group. A black chief executive of a major agency told his staff shortly after his employment that one of his major objectives was "to change the sex and the race of the professional staff." He went on to say that he did not anticipate discharging anyone but that as white men resigned or retired, they would be replaced by blacks and women. The result has been an increasing level of distrust within certain agencies. Another senior-level agency executive made the observation about a black colleague, "He is working the black agenda instead of the agenda of his board." The existence of formal and informal organizations of black staff members within units of the church bureaucracy and the organization of black bureaucrats across denominational lines is contributing to the increasing racial polarization within the church agencies as staff members sense that they cannot trust colleagues whose loyalty is elsewhere.

The sex and ethnic quotas for board and staff members are functions of an authoritarian system, not a collegial one. When rigid rules are required, the organization is saying that the constituency cannot be trusted to allow all of the elements in the membership to participate. It represents a lack of collegiality and mutual trust. In all probability many persons responsible for the present quota system saw it as a way of opening up the church leadership to a wider range of people, as a way of enhancing a collegial and participatory style. There is doubt whether a method that increases the degree of authoritarianism can produce these results.

In the final analysis a quota system means selecting an individual for a job on the basis of criteria irrelevant to performance. One denomination wanted a woman in a senior staff executive position, so one was hired. She was unable to perform satisfactorily and subsequently was discharged. She was employed because of sex but discharged for incompetence. The matter of fairness to the individual is called into question.

Agencies are likely to retain staff persons hired to fill quotas even when their performance is inadequate. A board member commented on the performance of an executive hired to fill a quota, "If he were not a member of a minority, we would have had him out of that job at least a year ago."

A major difficulty with the quota system is that it does not deal with individuals as persons. The individual is not what is important but the group to which he belongs. Under the old system, people were automatically excluded if they belonged to a particular group. It did not matter what skills and abilities the person might have possessed, membership in the group excluded him. Now we seem to have come full circle and again the individual is subsumed to the group. In this case the person is included because of some attribute of his particular population grouping. And again the individual is not important but rather his membership in the group. This point is made by sociologist Daniel Bell.

> The historic irony in the demand for representation on the basis of an ascriptive principle is its complete reversal of radical and humanistic values. The liberal and radical attack on discrimination was *based on its denial of a justly earned place to a person on the basis of an unjust group attribute*. That person was not judged as an individual, but judged—and excluded—because he was a member of a particular group. But now it is being demanded that one must have a place primarily because one possessed a particular group attribute. The person himself has disappeared. Only attributes remain. . . . We now find that a person is to be given preference by virtue of a role, his group membership, and the person is once again "reduced" to a single overriding attribute as the prerequisite for a place in the society. That is the logic of the demand for quotas.[2]

Fractured Relationships

Not all of the consequences of church restructure were anticipated. One unexpected result was a fracturing of the relationships between the bureaucracy and the regional judicatories and local churches.

The national agencies, unlike government and business, do

---

[2] Daniel Bell, *The Coming of the Post Industrial Society* (New York: Basic Books, 1973), p. 419.

not have local branch offices. Instead they have depended on a system of parallel organizations in each regional judicatory or local church. The persons who served on the local organizations were in effect part-time volunteer staff members for the national agencies.

To parallel the national Board of Social Concerns there was a Board of Social Concerns in each regional judicatory and a Social Concerns Committee in each congregation.

This system has had several important benefits. It provided a nationwide grass-roots organization which helped the agencies perform their tasks. Local people carried on educational programs, raised money, and engaged in other activities under the direction of the national agencies. A system of communication was provided for the denomination. By utilizing both formal and informal channel of communication, information could flow in both directions. The agencies had a readily available network by which they could get their messages to all parts of the denomination and receive information from the grass roots. Persons throughout the denomination, and particularly the staff persons in the regional judicatory, could interpret the needs and attitudes of pastors and church members to the national bureaucracy. The staff member in the national agency could keep in close touch with the constituents. A particularly significant benefit to the national bureaucracy of the system of parallel structures was that it provided a grass-roots political lobby that could work for their interest. From time to time every unit of the church agency comes under criticism. When this happens, the organization needs informed spokesmen who can represent its interests in the denomination's legislative assembly. Unless an agency can effectively present its case at the crucial time, it may be the victim of arbitrary and unfair action which may not only be detrimental to organization but to the denomination as a whole.

A major result of the restructuring has been to disrupt the

relationship between the national agencies and the other levels of the denomination. This has contributed to the increasing isolation of the bureaucrat and the growing alienation on the part of many church people.

There are several reasons why this has occurred. The first is that any major reorganization disrupts established patterns of relationships. Some staff members are reassigned; others resign or are discharged. The individual may find that the department whose services he has utilized may have a new name, may have been combined with one or more other units, or may have even been abolished. Thus the individual or group who wishes to use the services of the bureaucracy has to learn the new landscape. It might be assumed that within a couple years after the restructure was completed, the relationships between the bureaucracy and their constituencies would begin to return to normal. This has not been the case. One reason is that the agencies have not ceased tinkering with the bureaucratic machinery. The general restructure has been followed by various degrees of continued reorganization within the individual agencies. This situation prevents the reestablishment of helpful relationships with the constituents.

As the bureaucracy moves from a concept of a service agency for the churches to being an instrument of ministry and mission, the agency staff members (with the exception of those whose job is to raise money) see less reason to maintain a close liaison with the persons on the local level of the denomination. This will mean that bureaucrats will put more distance between themselves and the rank and file clergy and lay people.

The long-term effects of the fractured relationships will be harmful to both the bureaucracy and the denomination. Without extensive continued communication between the national staff and persons in the regional judicatories and local churches, the bureaucracy will increasingly turn inward. Attention will be focused on concerns of the staff that may or may not coincide with the needs or interests of people at the grass roots. The bureaucrats will become more isolated from their constituency and the constituents will have less understanding of the agencies, so the latent distrust that has always existed will surface.

One consequence of the turning inward is the continued emphasis on internal reorganization. When there are problems with purpose, with programs, or with the constituents, the easiest course is to rearrange the structure. This gives a sense of movement and produces some visible results (new titles and job descriptions or a different physical arrangement of the offices). Such a procedure is safe because it avoids confronting the critics or struggling with the hard issues.

A national church agency cannot survive as an effective organization if it allows itself to be cut off from its clientele. It may actually continue to exist for a period of years, becoming increasingly ingrown and ineffective. The chances are that it will simply be ignored by more and more people until at some point the denomination will decide that the agency is no longer worth the cost, and it will be abolished or merged with another part of the bureaucracy. This will occur quicker in times of economic stress than in prosperous periods. The fracturing of relationships and the cutting of the channels of communication has placed the national church bureaucracy in greater jeopardy than is generally realized.

The restructure of the national Protestant bureaucracy has already produced major changes in the denominations. More will occur in the years ahead. In the next section attention will be turned to the strategies for managing the church bureaucracy, beginning with predictions of the shape of things to come.

PART 4
STRATEGIES FOR MANAGING THE BUREAUCRACY

Chapter 9
The Shape of Things to Come

For more than a decade the major denominations have been making radical changes in their national bureaucracies. The process of restructure and the immediate results have been described in the preceding pages. The focus of this chapter will be on the future. It will consider what might be ahead for the national boards and agencies, given both the results of the restructure and the forces that are influencing the church bureaucracy.

Coordination

The restructure was to improve the coordination of the work of the national church bureaucracy. Duplication was the sin to be eliminated that would result in economy and efficiency. Structures to insure coordination were developed. The church today has more bureaucrats checking on other bureaucrats than at any previous time. There are no signs that the emphasis being given to coordination will diminish. The outlook is for a bureaucracy where greater attention is given to form and method than to the programs and services for which the organizations have existed.

The sin of the bureaucracy in the 1960s was not duplication

but a lack of perception of the areas where service could be effectively performed and where it could not. Every agency wanted to do the latest, most relevant thing. There was a tendency for all to jump on the current bandwagon. A result was often a duplication of irrelevant and futile effort. The restructure has not changed this. An example is how many church agencies rushed to make world hunger a major emphasis. While not depreciating the importance of this problem, not every church agency should be educating the same members about this issue.

Coordination has not been and will not be a substitute for creativity and imagination. Unless the boards of directors and the staff members they employ have these talents, the watchdog agencies will not instill them in the church bureaucrats. The formal monitoring will make the insecure staff more insecure. Greater attention may be given to doing things in the proper manner, having the correct forms and procedures, and carefully fencing off one's bureaucratic turf. This could detract from the development of creative programs and the clear definition of significant issues with which the church should deal.

Accountability

Restructure was to make the bureaucracy accountable to the denomination which created and supported it. There are three areas in which a church agency should be accountable. The first is ideological: It should reflect in its staff and activities an ideology generally in agreement with that accepted as normative by the church. This does not imply 100 percent agreement on every issue, but the bureaucracy should not espouse an ideology inconsistent with the theological tradition of the parent group.

A second area of accountability is programmatic. What the

153

agency does should be supportive of the objectives which its ideology implies. The objectives that the programs are to achieve should be clear so they can be tested against the theological assumptions.

A third area of accountability is fiscal. The agency should communicate to its constituency how it is using its money so that the programs it underwrites and the institutions and causes it subsidizes can be scrutinized against the goals which the denomination has assigned to the agency.

The demand for accountability will continue because it is clear that many church people are suspicious of bureaucrats. This condition existed before restructure, and the situation has not changed since. In the final analysis, accountability depends on the willingness of the board and staff members to be open with their constituents. Only when the agency personnel and the clergy and church members have some degree of agreement on the purposes and objectives of the agency is there likely to be a climate that encourages openness.

At present the problem of accountability is made more difficult, not only by the tension between bureaucrats and their constituents but by the complexity of the agencies, particularly the large ones. An annual report or a treasurer's statement may not be helpful in clarifying what an agency does. The demand for greater accountability by the agencies will continue so that the bureaucracy not only should be willing to be open but find ways of communicating with their constituents.

Centralization

The restructure of the bureaucracy resulted in the creation of fewer and larger agencies. Centralization of the boards and agencies was one of the major accomplishments in the

154

denominations that had their bureaucracy dispersed in several locations. Centralization is supported by such arguments as better internal communication, coordination, and control. Physical proximity can facilitate these if other factors are present. At this point in time it is not evident that the centralization has made a great deal of difference.

The creation of the large agencies by combining several smaller ones in the same location has important implications for the ways the agencies function now and in the future. In the case of the large superboards, denominations may have created an organization that is more difficult to manage and further removed from the constituency than that which was replaced.

A greater amount of time and energy is needed to run a large organization than a small one. Large agencies tend to develop a dynamic of their own. Running the machinery in the proper way takes on its own significance. The centralization seems to have increased bureaucratic overhead rather than reduced it.

The denominations may discover that if falling income forces further retrenchment, it will be easier to trim the large agencies than eliminate the smaller ones. The dropping of a department from a large organization can be accomplished with less outcry from the constituents than can the shutting down of a small agency. To reduce a small agency can mean closing it down, a fact obvious to its supporters. Dropping a department from a large agency may go unnoticed.

Centralization is an accomplished fact. There is no likelihood of the superboards being dismantled or the agencies dispersed. If the church income declines sufficiently, the large centralized agencies established in the early 1970s may become the small centralized agencies of the 1980s.

Pushing the Limits of Pluralism

The major Protestant denominations have always been pluralistic. Some have encompassed a broader range of persons and groups than have others, but each has numbered among its constituents some diversity of ideologies and social characteristics. Despite these differences, there has been an overarching loyalty to the denomination. People felt that the denomination was more important than the diverse groups within it. The advantages of being a part of the larger denomination more than offset whatever disadvantages accompanied the internal diversity. Pluralism was accepted, but the overall unity was affirmed as being of greater importance.

A trend emerging in the 1970s was the affirmation of pluralism as a positive characteristic. This was more than a recognition of the diversity within the churches. It was an attempt to reduce the growing internal conflict by affirming the different, and sometimes conflicting, elements within the denomination. This raises one of the most important questions for the church in the seventies. How much pluralism can a church stand without coming apart?

Loyalty to the church will always be in conflict with loyalty to one's subgroup when the purposes of each differ. The admonition that it is impossible to serve two masters is apropos. As the subgroups place the highest value on their own goals, they will become more polarized and membership in the denomination may be seen as an advantage or a handicap in the achieving of these goals.

The bureaucracy can be both a real and symbolic battlefield between the rival groups within the denomination. It is a real battlefield insofar as the agencies do represent for those who control them a degree of power, prestige, and patronage in the form of jobs and financial subsidies for programs and institutions. It is a symbolic battlefield as winning control of an agency clearly indicates to the constituents who the important people really are.

Even if the denomination does not come apart as a result of the increased internal conflict, the national agencies themselves may be the victims. The bureaucracies must depend on the voluntary support of a large majority of their constituents, not just a small portion of them. The agency which becomes the prize in a church political struggle between rival groups will hardly be able to count on the continued enthusiastic support of those who lose. The bureaucracy which becomes oriented only to a special-interest group is unlikely to find adherents among those persons who strongly disagree with its ideology and program.

Support and Income

The matter of support for the church boards and agencies will continue to be uncertain. Because the income is derived largely from the contributions of members of congregations, the future of the bureaucracy is linked to the financial health of the local churches and the confidence that the members have in the agencies.

There is ample evidence that people will support causes that are unambiguous, that capture their attention, and where it appears that their money will have a significant impact. The vast sums raised for world hunger are an example. Although feeding the world's population is a complex issue, people could easily understand emergency relief for famine-stricken areas and thus contributed generously. In contrast, there appears to be a growing skepticism about supporting ill-defined programs such as "empowerment." Many church people are unsure that an agency will use their contributions in worthwhile ways.

The trend in the income level of the church boards and

157

agencies has been downward. While this has varied among denominations and among agencies within the same denomination, retrenchment has been the characteristic of the 1970s. Furthermore, this trend will probably continue. There are four reasons that support this contention.

First, the church membership has been decreasing. The evidence is that people are not leaving the church but that new persons are not being recruited to replace those lost by normal attrition. Over the long run, this will have a negative effect on the financial support for the church agencies.

Second, national agencies will continue to have credibility problems with segments of their constituency. The orientation of the staff toward agency-based programs rather than services for the constituents has widened the gap between the bureaucracy and its supporters. There are no indications that the agencies are winning a greater degree of trust. The generation gap between the bureaucratic leaders who were products of the struggles of the sixties and the more recent parish-oriented seminary graduates will contribute to the problem in the period ahead.

A third factor is inflation. It costs more to operate the local parish and in many cases the offerings have not increased proportionally. Many churches have less discretionary money for causes outside the congregation. Local church expenses and programs will have first claim on the available funds.

Fourth, the competition between the national agencies and the regional judicatories for funds will increase with the regional groups having the advantage. During the optimistic expansionist days of the fifties and early sixties, many home-mission projects were started. The churches are more likely to give priority to supporting the local children's home or mission project than sending the funds to a national agency for use in some distant place. The church people know firsthand about the local project and have a direct sense of responsibility for it. This will make the difference.

158

The long-term picture for the national church bureaucracy seems to be one of financial stringency, of increasing struggles for a decreasing benevolence dollar, and of being forced to make hard priority decisions among worthwhile programs.

The Long-Term Struggle Over Quotas

It is normal for a practice, once initiated by a bureaucracy, to quickly become institutionalized by those persons who benefit from it. Thus the closing of the office for last year's big snow storm will be considered adequate precedent for allowing the employees to go home with the arrival of this year's first flurries. The adoption of agency board and staff quotas based on sex, race, and cultural groupings has become institutionalized.

While many persons who voted for formal quotas and who support informal quotas probably saw them as transitional, the evidence is that they will be a part of the church bureaucracy for the indefinite future. The persons who do or hope to benefit from the quotas will naturally attempt to perpetuate them. Any attempt to eliminate quotas will be met with strong opposition by those having a vested interest in their continuance. To try to alter the quotas will be interpreted as a step backward and be met with charges of sexism and/or racism.

The success of some groups in securing a quota for employment will result in the demand by other groups for their "just" share of the bureaucratic patronage pie. With a job quota on the ascribed characteristics of sex and race already established, the next step will be to demand preference on the basis of ideology. In this game any number can play. If women and members of ethnic and cultural minorities are entitled to positions on boards of directors and

159

agency staff, why not evangelicals, premillenialists, liberals, faith healers, and social activists?

The long-term insidious aspect of quotas is that they will subvert the function of the agency. The priorities tend to become internal with the major attention being given to the composition of the staff and their status. The task, program, or services to the constituents become secondary as who we are and how we do things takes precedence over what we do. The first step on the road to irrelevancy for a church agency is to give priority to internal matters. The present quota system is moving the church agencies in this direction.

The Increasingly Untenable Position of Staff

The distrust of the staff employed by the boards and agencies that has been observed throughout the restructure process still continues. There are no indications that this will change. The formal limitation of the time persons can be employed conveys the message that agency executives cannot be trusted. The long-term performance of the bureaucracy staff will be greatly affected by this continued expressed distrust and antagonism.

The present climate will have a negative effect on recruitment. The rewards of a position on the staff of a national agency may not be sufficient to enable the agency to hire the kind of persons most needed. The church has always been able to find persons who would accept difficult posts, including those with low salaries. Foreign missionaries are an example. Such persons were looked upon as exhibiting the Christian virtues of dedication, commitment, and sacrifice; of putting one's self second and the task of the church first. The church bureaucrat is perceived as having the opposite characteristics; of being self-seeking, building his personal

160

empire, and drawing a high salary that he really doesn't earn.

Furthermore, as the agencies themselves de-emphasize the function of the staff expert and move more to task forces made up of generalists, the relationship between staff and constituency will further deteriorate. Questions come to the agencies that require specific answers. As the church leaders across the country realize that their agencies cannot provide needed expertise, they will cease to call on them.

As the agencies have fewer staff experts, the level of constituency dissatisfaction will rise. As this occurs the staff tends to turn even more to internal bureaucratic matters, to attempt to swim in the swamp of the home office. Prospective staff members will be reluctant to jump in. The result will be an accelerating downward spiral of ineffectiveness and client dissatisfaction.

Continued Restructure

The restructure of the agencies with the acceptance of the reports of the special committees has not brought organizational stability to the church bureaucracies. There is a continual process of internal reorganization. Some of this has been made necessary as the agencies attempted to adjust to the new structure required by their denominations. The decreasing income has forced adjustments that have resulted in merging or eliminating parts of the bureaucracy. Furthermore, once the process of restructure has begun it is possible to continue. No longer are there decades of tradition and precedent to be overruled.

The time and attention given to changing structure, if it continues, can be destructive. A disproportionate amount of time can be given to internal organizational matters, time that will be taken from other tasks. As the process of restructure continues, the agencies will do fewer of the tasks for which they have been created. They will be less effective in terms of programs and services to their constituency.

A disproportionate amount of concern for structure can be a method of avoiding the difficult and more important matters. Structure is tangible, something with which people can feel comfortable. It is less threatening to consider the best city in which to relocate an agency or how to arrange the offices of the staff executives than it is to wrestle with the role the agency should perform in advancing the faith. There is a tangible reality about the organizational chart that is not necessarily present in a theological debate. The decisions regarding structure are less threatening to the persons who make them than are those dealing with the nature of the faith. The time and attention given to structure may be a way of avoiding the more difficult and fundamental issues. If the level of reorganization continuing throughout the second half of the 1970s equals that of the first half of the decade, it will be a clear sign that it is a technique for avoiding more important matters.

The Christian faith and the church are facing difficult and uncertain times. This is forcing those who call themselves Christians to reexamine their faith and theology that is derived from it. The next chapter will focus on the restructure of the national church agencies from a theological perspective.

Chapter 10

A Theological Perspective on Restructuring

In this chapter various specifics of the reorganization from a theological perspective will be considered. The church is a theological entity, called to share and proclaim a common faith in Christ as the body of Christ.

Christ is the center point in history, in persons's individual lives, and in the church. The revelatory and redemptive center of the church, Jesus Christ, is not an option for us. Christ is the way, the truth, and the life, the central given for the church's life. The church as the body of Christ is to speak to its theological identity. The biblical image of the church as a vital, dynamic organism is one way to express unity through diversity with God who has set Christ as the head of the church. The church is a divine organism, a community brought into being through the creative and redemptive work of God in Jesus Christ.

In an era long ago proclaimed secular, the church must maintain and reclaim its earthy vision as the body of Christ, Christ being the head—Christ above all. The church primarily is not a secular, social reality. Restructuring was a partial response to a crisis of faith. The crisis was soteriological (By whose name are we saved?) not managerial (How efficiently can the members carry out identified tasks?). The function of the church is not ultimately bureaucratic efficiency nor for that matter is function located in a particular kind of polity (How the church governs itself). The proper function of the church is to bear witness to the Lordship of Jesus Christ.

Hence church structure and form follow function—the hearing, sharing, proclaiming, and sacrificing in the name of Christ. To ask the world to set the agenda is to turn from the Christian vocation in God who "is faithful, by whom you were called into fellowship with his Son, Jesus Christ our Lord" (I Corinthians 1:9). This calling was muted in a preoccupation with form.

Surgery and the Body of Christ

Each denomination had a mandate to restructure. In the United Presbyterian Church in the U.S.A. and the Presbyterian Church in the U.S., the mandate focused principally on the national level. For the American Baptist Convention, structure, organization, and relationship within the life of the denomination demanded "adherence to traditional Baptist concepts of theology and polity." The United Methodist group was to address only the boards and agency organizational structure, and the Episcopalian committee received a similar mandate. For the Baptists this meant an overhaul from top to bottom; for the Methodists and Episcopalians only the horizontal structures and relationships at the national level received attention. For the Presbyterians, already committed to a reorganization of their synodical structures, the emphasis at the national level was to bring national agencies into functional relationship with the revised synodical and presbytery structural changes.

The organizational surgery worked most effectively with the American Baptists. The mandate was clear; both theology and polity were directly involved and, therefore, inseparable in the process. The Baptists began work with their self-understanding as belonging to the body of Christ and the desire to be more effective in their life together. The Presbyterians said in effect that their Constitution was their theological partner. The Methodists and Episcopalians were asked not to raise questions concerning the different levels of their denominational structure and the relationship between them. Thus the focus for all concerned, except the Baptists, was form and structure, not theology and polity. Such a separation of function and form, of theology and polity, is not possible. The resulting gradual shift in denominational emphasis from theology to program was predictable. Interest focused on very pragmatic, manageable, and objective details of corporation-type management issues. Attention to details of form and organizational, management goals is absolutely essential in any bureaucracy. But this shift toward technological objectivity about church operations made thinking about the church as the mystical body of Christ appear disjunctive, foreign, and immaterial. Mysticism and management are strange companions. But they are what the church is. The Baptists were more aware than others of the inseparableness of the form of the boards and agencies from their function in the mystical body of Christ. A decision for an administrative surgical procedure could not be separated finally from theological affirmations and decisions.

Thus, adequate restructuring requires a self-consciousness that declares that both theology and structure are involved. Structural and organizational questions cannot be resolved apart from theological questions. Theological problems dare not be ignored or displaced into organizational charts so only structural answers appear as significant.

All parts of the body of Christ were affected by restructure. The American Baptist imperative was to examine the entire church from top to bottom. This was, in fact, a far less frustrating surgery than the restrictions against considering any theological surgery. But the organic unity of the entire church body is experiencing post-surgery shock: the local churches, lower judicatories, the national boards, and theological assumptions. Some parts are more directly affected than others. But all are in fact altered by any major restructuring.

The church is a theological entity whose life is enriched by careful attention to whom and for whom its diverse parts relate and perform. Such an understanding must include relationships and performance of organizational activities as well as the miracle of the Incarnation, the deep mysterium of God's grace offered in Jesus Christ, and the sacramental communion through the Holy Spirit and the church. To set aside the basic theological affirmations, however they may be expressed, in a time of organizational crisis will exact a price of spirit and structure that may well leave the new structure in serious peril. The body of Christ, mystical and organizational, cannot live by management by objectives alone. It draws nourishment by every word that proceeds from God: the Bread of Life *and* the board of directors.

Life Blood of the Body of Christ

The body of Christ lives in ceaseless tension. The parts of the body are in dynamic relationship with one another and to the head, Jesus Christ. The church lives and grows in conflict, tension, fulfillment, frustration, and mystical union. No theological doctrines, no leadership style, no group should be discarded simply because the household of faith cannot always agree. Where there is life there is dynamic tension, a characteristic of any organism, including the body of Christ. This is a firm but forgotten New Testament description of the church and applies from its earliest days forward.

Illustrating shifts in the delicate balance of theology and polity in the churches was a *Christian Century* editorial,

"From TY to TICS."[1] The challenge was to acknowledge, celebrate, and encourage *openness* in the politics of the governance of a church group. While this openness should be applauded in its own right, the subtle implication is to focus church life increasingly on the relationships of polity and politics without critical review and assessment of the theological roots, perceptions, and realities. The actual tension in the church should not occur between polity and politics so much as between theology and politics.

The church and its "member groups" has learned from the radical politicization of life during the 1960s to become political or "intentional" about board and agency programs and in its national decision-making meetings. This shift occurred in the 1960s and probably will stay.

Accompanying the increased public exposure to programmatic statements, commitments, and funding is an increase in political activity in leadership selection. Keith Bridston has claimed that the selection of its leaders should be a public political church activity.[2] Critical attention should be given to candidates and their qualifications and credentials (theological, professional, social, ethnic, and geographical). The issue raised here is whether the church will be led by caucus power blocks or by the character of the leaders themselves.

Increased attention to and criticism of all church-sponsored programs has become political. Generally church staffs have employed statesmanlike patience to accommodate special-interest group claims. Eventually, however, theological and fiscal limitations will require the churches to acknowledge that they cannot and will not accommodate further special considerations.

Other political problems abound. The "go to seminary to

---

[1] "From TY to TICS," editorial, *Christian Century* (April 15, 1970), p. 435.

[2] Keith Bridston, *Church Politics* (New York: World Publishing Co. 1969).

find your faith" and the "try it you'll like it" attitudes by recruiters and students alike, less prevalent now than a decade ago, have nurtured questionable motivation for ordination. A corresponding concern was displayed by staff members of the Methodist Board of Missions that the church needed to retool to compete with the Peace Corps for youth.[3] Prospective seminary students, a church-related peace corps, or one of the myriad caucuses and pressure groups bring theological as well as political pressure to bear upon the church. The church needs to affirm the criticism that in fact it is not where every piece of the action is. The theological crucible known as the doctrine of ministry will grind finer in the future than during the recent past and present.

Another problem for the church's theology and polity is expressed in Michael Novak's *Rise of the Unmeltable Ethnics.*[4] He claims that America does not and is not likely to have a homogenized culture for the indefinite future. This means that the churches will have to struggle with ethnic, age, sex, regional, theological, and economic differences in its body in proclaiming God's word of love and redemption for persons and groups in their unmelted and unrefined state.

Another polity concern with theological implications is connectionalism. In restructuring it assumed new meanings. All denominations have acknowledged an operational connectionalism. Restructure produced considerable formal pressure to decentralize by relocating the center of gravity nearer the local church. The United Methodists and Episcopalians made no formal shifts here; but the Presbyterians located more power and authority in the synods (regional judicatories), and the Baptists reorganized power nearer the local congregation in their "Regions, States, and Cities" concept. Conversely, all groups shifted some responsibilities

---

[3]*Christian Century* (October 4, 1964), pp. 1273-74.

[4]Michael Novak, *The Rise of the Unmeltable Ethnics* (New York: The Macmillan Co., 1972).

toward the national level. The United Methodists did this in the General Council on Ministries, the Southern Presbyterians in the General Executive Board, the United Presbyterian Church in the U.S.A. in the General Assembly General Council, and the American Baptists in the Executive Council of the General Board. All groups self-consciously affirmed the principle of connectionalism: some movement toward local congregations, some toward national executive functions.[5]

The body of Christ image is a traditional theological term that was accumulating new meaning. Traditionally, Episcopal-oriented groups claimed centralized, national governance while congregation-oriented groups claimed local autonomy. Now the Episcopal governance groups will be giving up some of their traditional centralized power. The congregational governance groups will be surrendering some of their traditional local autonomy. There will be an increasing shift to the middle judicatories, the regionally oriented bodies for programming and funding. In medicine we find an analogy helpful in understanding this shift. The interlocking interdependency of the entire human system upon each individual part is truly remarkable, including the way larger systems compensate for injured tissues and organs. This understanding strengthens our contemporary use of biblical concepts and traditional theological images to affirm that the lifeblood of the body of Christ is our unity out of diversity, and diversity within unity. This neo-connectionalism should strengthen the organizational Body.

Core Theology: Closed and Open

It has been claimed throughout the study that restructuring was a crisis of faith to a far greater extent than a crisis of management style and bureaucratic efficiency. An underly-

---

[5] Lyle E. Schaller, "Connectionalism: The New Polity?" *Christian Century* (July 1, 1964), pp. 858-61.

ing reason for this crisis resides in a theological dilemma whose magnitude vastly surpasses the particular organizational frustrations of a dozen years or so. A core theology of American Protestantism has not been identified and received by popular church acclaim. There are some hints about the composition of such an effort. Those sect theologies indigenous to American soil are, by traditional theological standards, marginal or outside a church or theology whose basis is truly reformed, truly catholic, and truly evangelical. The indigenous groups, most prominently the Church of the Latter-day Saints and the Church of Christ, Scientist, emphasize an optimism toward people and the future and perceive a fluidity in God's relation with creation that does not exist similarly in European and fundamentalistic thought. In short, American theology is organized by "informal" theological categories that may be best expressed by process modes of thought. This basic world view or life orientation can be seen throughout the full spectrum of both clergy and laity.

It is beyond the scope of this study to do more than hint at this novel, constructive way of expressing the spirit of American theology. But, from the study of the bureaucracy, this need and direction of thought makes such a theological clarification and venture more imperative.

During restructure the theological crisis became intense. Truth and relevancy often were confused. Charles McCoy spoke of this as a docile adherence to European themes and a tendency to talk in closed circles.[6] This struggle was further illustrated by statements made by Charles P. Lutz of the World Council of Churches and Cynthia Wedel of the National Council of Churches. Lutz first argued,[7] and Wedel

---

[6] "The Plight of American Theology," *Christian Century* (July 11, 1962, pp. 859-61.

[7] "Middle America: Theologically Formed," *Christian Century* (March 18, 1970), pp. 323-25.

further developed his themes,[8] that middle America has a theology that is a confused blend of key Christian doctrines and three basic cultural values that need unlearning.

First, was the emphasis on human sin and corruption. The Vietnam War, Watergate, and church fiscal blunders suggest that this doctrine will remain intact among the populace. There is, however, a shift from a thorough-going doctrine of original sin to a doctrine of original ambiguity or potentiality: life can go either way, good or bad. But a shift to original righteousness is not in the theological cards. Thus we see some guarded, provisional optimism about effective, long-term benefits derived from social and institutional changes and, therefore, some diminution in the confusion over cultural optimism and theological pessimism.

Second, was a doctrine of salvation that emphasized the centrality of grace. Perhaps less shift occurred here than in the theological anthropology. With the mellowing influence of contemporary reformed theologians, God's grace is perceived as not simply an antidote for sin. Thus, both God and man affirm the judgment; but grace is generously given and received. Grace is more than a super-objective decision rendered in a court case but an openness to the loving expression of God's grace freely given. However grace occurs, a self-conscious affirmation and confirmation is needed, and this cannot be hid under the bushel. The Christian is one of God's own choosing and actively participates in that choosing. The need and claim for public affirmation of God's grace is less confused now than early in the period.

Third, is the immutability and unchangeableness of God. We find some renewed rigidity here in concept but less in percept. During the God-is-dead days of the mid-sixties, the so-called middle Americans received very little help, sup-

[8]"The Church and Social Action," *Christian Century* (August 12, 1970), pp. 959-62.

port, and reassurance from mainline Protestant theologians. That abandonment will not quickly be forgotten in the discussion about the reality of God. There is little formal meeting of the minds on this issue to date.

Some *un*learning and *re*learning have occurred during the period for both lay and professional theologians. Some discussions are more open; some more closed. One would be remiss in failing to observe that the behavior of the bureaucracy and the professional theologians themselves indicates that Lutz's "middle American" was not further off-base or confused than the theologians and bureaucrats.[9] Marty expressed that experience of judgment and repentance "Clay Feet Clear Up to Our Navels."[10]

Use of European themes required similar clarifications and reassessment. Bonhoeffer, in his popular appeal, represented one who had fallen from a closed, aristocratic society into grace. Yes, the world came of age. But in the United States and among Studs Terkels' working class it had been coming of age with the genocide of slaves, a civil war, and the myth of the middle class long before Hitler with his gas chambers and prison camps. A major difference was the American tendency to wink at secularism for more than a century, while Bonhoeffer *et al.* were overwhelmed all at once. Existentialism, theology of hope, Marxist Christianity, and other themes which stimulated the quest for theological truth and mutual conversation were provocative and enlightening. But these were not the dominant themes in American Protestant churches.

Any core of theology in American Protestantism is both more basic and more elusive than had been appreciated. One constructive theological refinement to emerge from the church bureaucracy was an increasing awareness of the

---

[9]Martin E. Marty, *The Fire We Can Light* (New York: Harper & Row, 1973). See chap. 6, "Nearsighted Leaders, Blind-Sided, and Recovery."

[10]*Ibid.*, chap. 4.

sociality of human life: Vietnam, Watergate, Social Security contributions and benefits, interstate highways, the gross national product, television networks, credit cards, the energy crisis, pollution of earth and air and sea, and the new connectionalism in church bureaucracy. In sum, the agony of restructure revealed the lack of a constructive theological base for church forms. Restructuring carried some constructive theological import. It pointed toward the emergent need for identifying and clarifying the parameters of a theology for American Protestantism, including its bureaucracy and middle America.

Boards and Agencies: Symbols of Theology

Public hearings focused on efficiency, historical obligations, cost reduction, decentralization, and a change from telling to enabling. Earlier it was questioned whether the goals of efficiency, lower costs, decentralization, and so forth were accomplished. The answer is probably not. The most significant theological symbol, however, did not emerge from these particularities. It was simply that the bureaucracy was confused about truth and relevancy, and this theological uncertainty was translated into structural "uptightness." Restructuring may have created boards and agencies that were all too bureaucratic in their managerial accountabilities but confused in their theological responsibilities.

The boards represented certain discrete theological beliefs and restructuring influenced those values in their particularities but not in their wholeness. The structure became the church's theological witness and symbol although it was not pointing beyond itself to the whole body of Christ. Hence certain programs and persons and their theology prospered under one agency's banner while other programs and persons and their theology, under other boards, had leaner times. In

173

the political confusion and tension, certain agencies were favored and others apparently neglected or punished. All church bureaucracy is pluralistic in its structure and theology. If these are not carefully balanced disastrous consequences ensue.

The superboards are like the SST (Super Sonic Transport). Their blueprint versions far exceed the performance characteristics of any previous model. But they are too large, too powerful, too autonomous, too cumbersome to handle, and too expensive, and they move too high through their trajectory. By contrast, the body of Christ metaphor calls for more emphasis in the humbler regions, the middle and lower judicatories. The church is called by traditional theological categories to affirm both the person and work of Jesus the Christ. This means that a superboard needs its identity but must work for the Body. This requires spending time with people actively participating in the middle- and local-level church life of the Body.

In the interviews with staff, questions were asked about personal activities and responsibilities in local churches. The response was uneven; some were self-consciously and sacrificially active in a local congregation. For some to have the question asked was an affront; for others, schedule made consistent local church leadership involvement difficult. The conclusions were that the personal schedule demands could be a real problem, and to limit participation may have been wise in the light of current national-level work responsibilities. But, it must be noted that busy church executives are no more pressed by schedules and commitments than are executives in many corporations. The church may discover from a careful examination of its own staff commitments and priorities one of the reasons for general membership decline. Active executives have difficulty settling down for local church participation. Another observation is related to the significant number of staff who had put a theological,

174

cultural, and life-style chasm between their world and the local church. There seemed too much distance, too much pushing away from the more humble parts of the body of Christ. The superboards may well be the SST of the church with many advantages but at an excess operating expense that leaves a trail of negative residue that does not build up the Body.

Finally, there is the bureaucratization of all the boards' and agencies' work. One motive in restructure was to eliminate the overlay of interboard committees, to reduce if not eliminate political empire-building enjoyed by various staff persons through informal executive level peer groups. Another was the desire to break up the ward-style politics of the agency heads by which a staff person in one area (missions, evangelism, youth, urban work, worship, etc.) developed a network of apostles and informants so that certain persons and areas could be ahead of others in the line for rewards. The restructure attempted to break up these alliances, to dismember the informal councils, and to put asunder personal empires. The organization was to be run by objectives, computers, and professional managers.

An immediate result was to recruit the "bureaucratic eunuch," a kind of thoroughly domesticated churchman. Theologically this introduced or retained a high level of distrust and suspicion among the boards and agencies personnel. Far surpassing any earlier fear that the denominational general executive-type group (GCOM, GSGC, GEB, GEGB, and ECNC) would become a curia were the proliferation of minicuriae whose task was to see that the agencies ran a tight ship. Such close accountability indicated a level of distrust and gracelessness that may have the long-term effect of attracting the intellectual and spiritual eunuch to work in the bureaucracy.

Another fact in tight administrative control relates to the dynamics of human behavior in general. People are social

175

creatures and being social involves both formal and informal relations. The more carefully the formal ties are programmed, processed, and charted, the greater pressure the staff feels to invest its real ego and values in informal groups and relationships, Informal cliques, a communications grapevine, peer councils, and empire-building will emerge, not to subvert the bureaucracy, but because it is human nature to participate in informal, trusting, graceful, and satisfying groups. No bureaucracy can long tolerate the tyranny of an informal power elite, neither can it be effective by trying to suppress and/or eliminate informal groupings. The lax and thoughtless informal group invites the charlatan and con artist. The uptight formal group invites the impotent and uncreative. Currently there appears a need for a higher level of trust to let people function responsibly and creatively.

The current board and agency configuration appears too tight; generally the body of Christ is still struggling to facilitate the mutual growth of the church.

Priestly Authority and Pop Art

George Benson, an active Episcopal layman, psychiatrist, and psychoanalyst, commented on the problem of pastoral authority.[11] Benson has close ties with the national organizations most involved in training pastoral counselors (the American Association of Pastoral Counselors and the Association of Clinical Pastoral Education). He is directly acquainted with theological and pastoral education, specializing in developing counseling skills. He intended his observations to apply to students, pastors, and professionals in the denominational bureaucracy. He claimed that being a

---

[11] "Psychoanalytic Notes on the Disavowal of Priestly Authority," *Christian Century* (May 28, 1969), pp. 738-41.

representative of the church—whether ordained or lay—
rightly carries a priestly authority. Symbolically, a bureaucratic agency is a crosssection of the church. As an
ambassador for the church, the bureaucracy assumes a
legitimate and necessary priestly authority in its words and
deeds, in all its activities. Benson observed the tendency of
priests and parishioners to back away from claiming the high
calling which they have in Jesus Christ and his church.

> I conclude therefore that today's problem as to priestly authority
> is neither a new problem nor a product of a 20th century faith
> crisis. It is an old problem. Telling it like it is has never been easy.
>   The Christian, and above all the Christian minister can dare to
> look at the darkness around him and the darkness within him; can
> dare to face up to the despair which seems to dog man's finest
> efforts as well as his worst; can dare to tell it as it is because he
> knows that now as always, when he has been willing to face the
> darkness, he finds the light of the Love of God. I have
> paraphrased Scripture not because it is beautiful poetry but
> because it is a verifiable fact that people who will face darkness
> find light. [12]

Reluctance to claim or to outright disavow that calling and
authority, notes Dr. Benson, condemns both priest and
parishioner to the mediocrity of being nice guys. Neither the
priestly function of the bureaucracy nor the mystical body of
Christ can be disavowed and remain healthy. Here "priestly"
includes prophet and priest functions; they are coterminous
in contrast to any secular authority of the church.

Failure to accept and claim that priestly authority in the
bureaucracy has resulted in a vast array of mediocre,
defensive, and secular manifestations. Programs have been
promoted that would make the church a peace corps, a
counseling center, a high-risk loan institution, and, perhaps
most symbolically, a consulting firm. The change in the
bureaucracy work-style from doer to enabler has many

---

[12]*Ibid.*, p. 740.

salutary benefits. But in light of Benson's analysis one has to question the underlying theological dynamics in the move from priest to nice guy, from doer to enabler, from authority to consultant.

Lower judicatories and local churches look to the national agencies for answers. Some of the expectations may be unrealistic, but generally the problems are specific, technical, and need a direct answer. There is a reasonable claim for a knowledgeable and helpful response. Direct answers can be given without being authoritarian. In fact, those most preoccupied with someone else's authoritarianism are least secure in their own authority. Hence, the shift from authority to consultant–enabler may have a significant constructive psychological rationale but may represent a negative theological or priestly motivation to "tell it like it is," to say yea or nay and to be accountable to the whole body of Christ.

Priestly authority is found in the High Priest Jesus Christ and bestows authority to say yes and no and mean it and yet be gracious. The nice guy, however, does not participate openly and freely in that transcendent authority graciously bestowed. The latter gains authority through a secondary process of detachment, the bureaucrat as enabler, consultant, or process person.

There are two constructive conclusions: (1) The movement is away from excessive individualistic authority to legitimate priestly authority, and (2) there is a countermovement toward legitimate authority, away from investing authority in secular society or the pop-art motif of baptising every breeze of cultural novelty as important for the church.

A denomination within the body of Christ cannot be run by an ecclesiastical mafia gathered in the denominational equivalent of the smoke-filled room. Nor can the church be run by a vast conglomerate consisting of nice-guy consultants from the outside. During the restructure period authority

178

fluctuated between these extremes. Was the bureaucracy run by a dirty dozen or by a nobody dressed as a paid consultant? The church will continue to have both elements influencing its life. Which will become more influential? At this juncture the denominational bureaucracies appear unable to claim one style decisively over another.

Chapter 11
Creation Out of Chaos

Despite the time, effort, and money that the Protestant denominations spent on the restructure of their national bureaucracies, the process still continues. Some of the changes are adjustments in the new organizational forms. Others reflect the high degree of dissatisfaction by some church leaders with the way the new structure is working. The churches seem to be in a period in which tinkering with the ecclesiastical machinery is the order of the day.

This chapter will focus on several issues that are central to any attempt of a denomination to restructure its national bureaucracy. No church can avoid this when it embarks on the task of designing a new organization.

Theological Strategy and Managerial Practices

The basic theme of the study is that the restructuring in the 1960s and early 1970s was the result of a crisis of belief and therefore of theological strategy. From the diversity and chaos of the period little unity emerged to provide a clear theological position from which the churches could develop a clear theological strategy for their activities and their organizations. In the denominations were separate agencies and boards, each needing its own plans, goals, and strategies. At the same time, each church should have a unified strategy

180

or overall design. Various potential activities (missions, curricula, local church nurture and education, worship, higher education) are the building blocks or structures that make unity possible. But only those persons who do the activities will make the possible unity a reality. The ideology and general perspective of the executives, for example, provide them with a sense of unity in their diverse activities.

Belief systems blend into technology. Technology properly understood is more than engineering or industrial production. *Techne*, the Greek root word of technology means "useful knowledge" or "organized skill." The specific technology of a board or agency is its common core of unity. Some combination of useful knowledge (theology) and organized skill (agency function) forms the hub of the wheel, the core for any unity. This relationship of knowledge and skill provides both the possibility of getting things done and a common language for the denomination.

The skills and knowledge valued by the designers of the new structure tended to be oriented more to the skills and knowledge of specific bureaucratic forms and functions (church development, minority empowerment, urban work, colleges, loan programs, etc.) and not to "theology technology." This common core, essential for unity, was not consistently maintained. The structural questions were reversed. The constituency or marketing question is not, "How do we structure for what we do?" Instead the real issue is, "What is the *value* the constituency pays for?" This must be followed by the technology question, "What can we do with great skill and high distinction?"[1]

At first this may appear to jeopardize the entire restructuring process. If the leaders are told the values of the church, where is the place of constructive and creative

---

[1] Peter Drucker, *Management* (New York: Harper & Row, 1974). See chap. 57, "Building Unity Out of Diversity," pp. 696-700.

leadership? Surely some values currently held by the church-at-large ought to be changed. But identifying the *actual* and *stated* values would allow the bureaucracy openly to participate in relocating those values central to the church's life. These values and beliefs would not necessarily be solely what the bureaucracy does.

There is a theological technology common to the entire denominational membership, including its bureaucracy, that cannot be set aside in restructure. For a common technology to exist for the church, both theory-focused (theology) and skill-focused bureaucratic technologies must be present. Properly, bureaucracy restructuring cannot be accomplished without addressing the theory-focused questions. In light of the relationship of theory and skill, the question for the church bureaucracy is, "What can we do with great skill and high distinction?" There are some activities that the bureaucracy can and cannot do with great skill and high distinction.

Theology and skill are interwoven in the bureaucracy. But the perceived disparity between national-level and local-level theology was such that theological questions in general were not raised explicitly. Instead of working to affirm a "common language" of theological technology, the bureaucracy during the 1960s looked outside the church for its theology technology. It was found in the slick secular streets, the moody fads, and the diverse language of the caucus groups. The coming financial crunch and the caucus rhetoric impelled the bureaucracies to run for cover, to weather out fiscal localism and ideological conservativism. But the organizational and theological questions still lurk in the background: (1) What value does the customer pay for? (2) What can be done with great skill and distinction? Restructuring was the capstone to a period of extreme diversity, confusion, and fluidity. Theology as a theory-focused activity was not joined as fully as the skilled-focused activities. Consequently, the common core was eccentric or off to one side. The common language had become a nontheological language whose etymology was clearly outside the language of the church.

In sum, future efforts to restructure limited segments of the church bureaucracy or an entire denomination will require both theory-focused and skill-focused study. Theology technology is as vital a part of the common core of church life as is program technology. Without this there is no common language and no common life in the body of Christ.

Decentralization

Any discussion about reorganization will introduce the question of decentralization. The Baptists and Presbyterians did more than talk about the problem. They developed decentralized entities: for the Baptists, regions, states, and cities; for the Presbyterians, regional synods.

There are several general questions: (1) Is there an organizational entity with the power to do a given activity with great skill and high distinction? (2) What is unique and opposing about the central and the satellite agency that creates an organizational mandate to locate a given activity in a "lower" (regional) and not a "central" (national) agency?

Lower judicatories that mirror the central agency in function and structure have no autonomy or individuality and are doomed to be branch offices. If they are to be more than a "pipeline" they have to have their own autonomy, they have to provide a unique service, and the activity itself must differ from that of the national offices. To decentralize involves a unique location of real organizational power and values (personnel, expertise, funds). To be effective, the decentralized agency cannot fit ideologically and temperamentally in another level of the bureaucracy.

Decentralizing in some cases will have positive values, but

183

these must go beyond rhetoric and be based on autonomous power. A concern in any consideration of decentralization is whether the church should be in this particular area at all. The real issue may be that a particular activity no longer belongs in the church bureaucracy. A national agency may discontinue a program by simply transferring it to the regional judicatories.

In restructuring there was movement in both directions. Some activities were centralized and others decentralized. It has been observed that there are two management styles in bureaucracy.[2] (1) The management by objective style is most effective where the objectives pertain to highly objectifiable goals: salaries, pensions, loans, scholarships, research, building construction, curricular design, hospitals, and church extension. These activities tend to be mechanical and therefore inherently objective. (2) The management-by-negotiation style is most effective where the objectives pertain to that elusive activity, the human being: local church life, recruitment and ordination, worship, ecumenics and evangelism. Of course, these are general and not pure categories. Many activities are a combination of both.

Activities which are more objective generally can be centralized more readily and effectively than those which consistently require negotiation. In the negotiating style, the nearer the persons most likely to be affected in negotiations, the better. "Nearer" here carries several meanings: geographically, ideologically, ethnically, or culturally. What are the available resources (persons and locations) to enter the relationship with skill and distinction? It may be that no combination of locations and persons will speak to the values people are paying for and the promise anticipated from that activity. If the appropriate resources are not available decentralization will be ineffective and the church cannot

---

[2]*Forbes* (July 15, 1975), pp. 57-58.

enter into that particular area. In short, if an activity does not work or its promise is not being fulfilled, moving the activity to another structure (up, down, or sideways) will probably not improve the situation and could make it worse.

Finally, the role of the executive must be considered in a country made five hours wide and two and one-half hours deep by jet travel. The question of *travel* and *image* relates to the executive's style of ministry. Some executive functions need centralized activities. Minimal travel is involved, and the image of the executive is not an essentially persuasive factor in the success of the activity. People have conflicting views about persons in the denomination who have high visibility and are perceived as remote from them. They like to identify with a prominent leader, and the executive from the national office is considered more important than the person in the regional judicatory. Decentralization is essentially a political decision, somewhat related to regional envy or the desire to keep as much power and prestige as near home as possible.

An underlying issue is the *amount* and *ease* of travel for the staff. Does the travel itself enhance or detract from the value the constituents are paying for? How can the executive travel and negotiate with great skill and high distinction?

Decentralization is ever on the lips of the reformer and bureaucrat. But neither centralization nor decentralization has intrinsic merit. The question is, How do centralized or decentralized activities respond to the values being paid for? And if the activities appear to require excessive movement in either direction, to what extent should the national level of the church be involved?

Orientation and Self-Image

The restructure of the church bureaucracy has as one of its goals the creation of agencies that will perform certain

185

defined functions. These may include the role of change agent in the larger society, carrying out ministries in behalf of the denomination and providing specialized services to the congregations, the clergy, or some combination of the above. The persons responsible for the restructure of the agencies had some concept of what the final product was to look like and what it was expected to do.

A reorganization of the national Protestant boards and agencies, however, begins with the raw material of the existing structure. This includes the traditions, functions, and programs of the present agencies, the board and staff members, the institutions supported, and even the property owned. A "new" organization is created by changing, merging, rearranging, and eliminating parts of the present structure. It is impossible to wipe the slate clean and create a bureaucracy *de novo*. The orientation and self-image of the old agencies are mixed into the new structure with the final product not being completely predictable. An assessment of the self-image of the bureaucracy that is being replaced would facilitate the task of designing a new organization that would perform in the desired ways.

The orientation and self-image of an agency is the sum of the ways the directors and the professional staff perceive their task and the agency's tasks. The directors hire the executives and charge them with certain responsibilities. If the executive's understanding of the work of the agency does not coincide with that of the directors, conflict is inevitable. The executive will either change, be discharged, or dominate the directors. The changing of an agency requires either that people change their orientation and self-image or that different persons be employed. Much that was accomplished by the extensive church restructuring could have been attained by changing key personnel. Some reorganization seems to have had the replacement of certain staff members as one motivation.

A continuing problem is how the denomination can maintain a supervisory control over its agency employees. There is no easy answer. The responsibility rests with the elected members of the boards of directors. These are the persons who must determine whether the orientation and the performance of the employees are adequate and consistent with the purposes of the agency. They must make the difficult judgment concerning not only the competency of the staff, but whether they are fulfilling the mandate of the agency. The proliferation of agencies for coordination and control is an indication that church leaders feel that the boards of directors are not exerting adequate control over the agencies.

In the rush to relevancy and the desire to be on the "cutting edge" in the late 1960s and early 1970s, the church bureaucracy became prisoners of the mass media. The agencies felt compelled to work on whatever was perceived to be the immediate problem. To do less would have been inconsistent with their self-image of social change agent. An example of this thinking occurred when an agency executive called in a staff member and said, "I think the civil rights movement is dead; we have got to find another issue. Would you give some thought to planning a possible church campaign against political extremism?"

Not every church agency can or should be attempting to deal with what the staff has read in the morning paper. Some must be assigned to the routine but necessary tasks that must be done if the church is to carry on its range of ministries. The routine can also be necessary to achieving the greater good. These more prosaic agencies need to be protected and supported in a media-oriented society. Not every agency should have the same task or self-image.

This orientation and self-image are the results of value judgments that individuals make. Or to put it another way, they are based on the theological assumptions to which the church leaders subscribe. And any change in the church must

187

ultimately come to rest on what the persons involved and the agencies they represent believe to be important.

Political Power: Symbolic and Real

In considering the political strength of a denomination, it is necessary to clarify the differences between symbolic and real power. Generally, church political power displayed in the public arena is symbolic and not real. The church uses symbolic power by giving (or not giving) its approval to social policies and actions by other groups in the society.

In the civil rights struggle of the sixties, the churches put their weight and witness behind the powers pushing for increased civil rights. The outcome proved fruitful, and the churches received appropriate appreciation. The church's power in that struggle was symbolic. The real power lay in the disenfranchised, oppressed blacks who were beginning to move against racist attitudes and power. The forces of resistance were located deep within certain economic, political, and social mores and folkways. Those blacks leading the movement utilized the clergy to legitimize the moral and spiritual dimensions of the struggle. But without black leaders and some willingness by the Southern white power structure to move, the involvement of white clergy and national church staff would have been of little significance.[3]

But when it came to the church's entrance into the banking business such as MELIC, the Methodist loan program for small businesses, it overstepped its power base by attempting to move from symbolic to real power.[4] The church assumed incorrectly that it could act effectively as a financial power. Since churches traditionally have expressed their

---

[3] Warren Carr, "Notes from an Irrelevant Clergyman," *Christian Century* (July 10, 1963), pp. 879-80. See earlier, p. 51, note 16.

[4] See discussion of MELIC in chapter 6, "Fiscal Fiascoes."

symbolic power with gifts, grants, and aid to diverse groups and causes, the passing of funds directly into society was not the central power problem. In the symbolic use of money, funds were consumable or payable as service in one form or another. Thus, there was not the need for skill-focused technology such as providing technical advice to the borrowers and collecting the interest and principal due. In attempting to exert real power, these skills were essential. The question that the bureaucracy should have asked itself initially was, Do we have the power, expertise, and willingness to collect these loans in their entirety, including the use of lawsuits? *Who* in the bureaucracy will do that with great skill and high distinction? Because that type of question was not asked, the bureaucracy entered upon a course of action that it lacked the power to accomplish.

The *values* the constituents were paying for in this instance were not the economic development of exploited and oppressed peoples. The value at issue was the permanence of reserve funds to be used over a long period for the mission work of the churches. With that value in mind, the agency should have been especially attentive that the long-term, or short-term, investment *goals*, as values, be preserved. It would have taken more power and leadership strength to have come to the conclusion that this development in mission, while desirable, was *not* for the church. Peter Drucker has commented about this kind of problem:

> They saw the skills that "fitted" but not the ones they lacked. And a corollary is the question, "And what old technology do we · need to abandon or play down because it does not fit the new products, services, or markets?"[5]

The symbolic presence of the church is to recruit and legitimize additional and real support from outside the

---

[5] Drucker, *Management,* p. 703.

bureaucracy and the church itself. The unique functions and limitations of the power of the church as symbolic and real should not be confused. When a church agency attempts to exercise real power in an area where it has only symbolic power, the results can be disastrous.

Counting the Cost

A factor that should be seriously considered by denominational leaders before embarking on the largely uncharted seas of restructure is the cost. The price of reorganizing the church bureaucracy has been high, probably much higher than was either anticipated at the outset or even realized after the process was more or less complete.

The rush to restructure by the denominations in the late sixties and early seventies was not accompanied by a careful counting of the costs. The assumption was made that the old agencies were inefficient, and engaged in expensive duplications of programs and services. The new structure was to be more efficient and more economical than the old. The special committees and commissions charged with restructuring the churches did not do a careful analysis of the old agencies. No one has done a study of the costs of the new structure, but it is not evident that the new is or will be either more efficient or economical than was the old.

The price of restructure is paid by the denominations in several ways. The first is the cost in money. Included are the direct expenditures of the committee that had the responsibility for designing the new plan of organization. Although this was a substantial sum of money, it was the least costly aspect of denominational restructure. The indirect financial costs far exceed the actual expenditures of the special committees. The members themselves received no pay so those who were pastors or judicatory officials had their salaries carried by their congregations or by the denomination. The restructure committees called upon agency staff for various services. Other staff members, particularly the executives, lobbied for their particular concerns with their agency paying the costs. Furthermore, the amount of bureaucratic staff time that went into worrying about, plotting for and against, and learning to operate the new structure was considerable. Finally, the time and energy given to restructure by denominational employees represented a substantial cost to the denomination in other work not done and other services not performed.

The expenses of implementing the new structures were enormous. Offices were moved distances that ranged from across the hall to across the country. Employees were dismissed, which required termination benefits. Professional staff members were relocated, but the secretarial and other support personnel tended to be unwilling or unable to move. Thus, years of valuable experience were lost while new persons had to be trained. The cost to the church was in the lost productivity of the agency as it went through an extended shakedown cruise.

The second cost was to people. Restructure resulted in the dislocation of persons. Staff at all levels have had their lives disrupted. This, of course, varied with the individual. Some persons have paid a higher price than others. The executive may find it inconvenient to relocate to a distant city, but he can do so. The middle-aged secretary with an invalid parent and twenty-four years of service to the church agency may not have that option. The pastor with a son about to enter college who has served on an agency staff for ten years may find his dismissal difficult to understand or accept.

Restructure for the employees involved is a very personal matter that can alter their lives. Such persons are required to pay a high price. The denomination should not rationalize that the separation benefits are better than a business would normally provide, or that is a chance one takes when accepting a position in church bureaucracy. The church asks a depth of commitment from people. When it asks for sacrifices it should see that the probable end results have a chance of being commensurate with the cost that some people must pay.

Finally, there is a theological price attached to the restructure of the denominational boards and agencies. The church bureaucracy is built on certain implicit, if not explicit, doctrines. The change in structure will inevitably bring with it ideological shifts. The motivation for the reorganization represents a change in the present theological system with the adherents of the new seeking to implement their values through changing the church structure.

The theological cost comes in the dislocation of the ideological base on which the agencies rest. Pastors and lay people become unsure of the rationale for the bureaucracy. They may not be clear about the goals of the agency or how to relate to them. They are uncertain how its ideology may conflict with their values. If the restructure process continues over a long period of time, the constituents never know where the agency is. This ideological instability is one of the costs that must be counted when restructure is being considered.

There are times when the denominations may need to make radical changes in their bureaucracy. Those who make the decision to do so must beware lest they become caught in the trap of the individual who buys a car with no money down and "easy monthly payments." They, like the purchaser, may find the long-term costs and unexpected charges both larger and different than were anticipated.